SEC
FOOTBALL'S
GREATEST
GAMES

SEC
FOOTBALL'S GREATEST GAMES

THE LEGENDARY PLAYERS, LAST-MINUTE PRAYERS, AND CHAMPIONSHIP MOMENTS

ALEX MARTIN SMITH

Guilford, Connecticut

An imprint of The Rowman & Littlefield Publishing Group, Inc.
4501 Forbes Blvd., Ste. 200
Lanham, MD 20706
www.rowman.com

Distributed by NATIONAL BOOK NETWORK

British Library Cataloguing in Publication Information available

Library of Congress Cataloging-in-Publication Data

Names: Smith, Alex Martin, 1992- author.
Title: SEC football's greatest games : the legendary players, last-minute prayers, and
    championship moments / Alex Martin Smith.
Other titles: Southeastern Conference football's greatest games
Description: Guilford, Connecticut : Lyons Press, an imprint of The Rowman & Littlefield
    Publishing Group, Inc., [2018] | Includes index.
Identifiers: LCCN 2018018413| ISBN 9781493032914 (hbk.)
Subjects: LCSH: Southeastern Conference—History. | Football—Southern States.
Classification: LCC GV958.5.S59 S65 2018 | DDC 796.332/630975—dc23 LC record available
at https://lccn.loc.gov/2018018413

Printed in the United States of America

CONTENTS

PART 1: THE GAMES THAT CHANGED THE SOUTH

The South's most famous tower did not cast its shadow upon Atlanta, Jacksonville, or New Orleans.

It rose only 33 steps above the practice field at the University of Alabama in Tuscaloosa, and it was occupied by one man: the Bear. Former Alabama coach Paul "Bear" Bryant stood atop the metal structure throughout two-plus decades of Crimson Tide dominance. It was a symbol of power, and it sent holy shivers through one Green Bay Packers scout in the summer of 1975.

Bill Curry, a center who had played at Georgia Tech before snapping the football to NFL legends Bart Starr and Johnny Unitas, was in his first season with the Packers front office when he traveled to Tuscaloosa to watch the latest Tide prospects. By that time, Bryant and Curry were acquaintances. But that familiarity couldn't keep Curry from shaking when Bryant called down to him from his tower. It was, Curry said, "the voice of God coming out of the sky."

"Bill," the Bear said. "Why don't you come up here where you can see something?"

The scout didn't waste a second.

"God almighty, that blew me away," Curry said. "I go scrambling up those spiral steps and stand up there in the heavens with God himself."

More than four decades later, Curry recounted this moment to me while I conducted interviews for a feature on the competing legacies of Bryant and current Alabama coach Nick Saban.

Bryant's and Saban's résumés rest atop the offerings of thousands of other coaches who have tried and failed to reach the pinnacle. Curry himself was the second man charged with following in Bryant's footsteps as Alabama football coach in the 1980s (Ray Perkins was the first). Curry took the Tide to the Sugar Bowl but was effectively pushed out near the turn of the decade.

"When I first got to Alabama, I thought I was worldly wise," he said. "I had spent a lot of time in the NFL. I had been through the players' strike. I was a president of the players' association. And I'd played in a bunch of Super Bowls, so I thought I knew all about big-time football.

"I was wrong. Big-time football is where it's the most important thing in life. All day. Every day. That's what you have at Alabama."

Look around the Southeastern Conference, and you'll find many similar cultures. Loyalists at Auburn, Georgia, and LSU (to name a few) have been preaching the healing power of college football for several decades.

In 2018 the SEC is the gold standard. Any recruiting service will tell you that Southeastern preps are a cut above their counterparts from different regions. These players have helped Southeastern teams win nine of the past twelve national title games and appear in two others. Thanks to those victories and some visionary off-field leadership, Southeastern schools share a ludicrous combined profit that has resulted in not only state-of-the-art athletic facilities, but vastly improved academic facilities on campus as well.

The conference recently adopted the marketing slogan "It just means more."

For those who wonder why, author Ray Glier went back to the 1800s for an answer in *How the SEC Became Goliath*: "The Civil War had crushed the ego of the South. The North was more urbanized and industrialized. It's why the North won the war and the South wanted to raise the level of its game. Football was part of the formula. The South finished second once before. Ever since, it has been determined to finish first."

In my conversation with Curry, the former Alabama coach posited a similar thesis.

"You need to understand the southern male personality," he said. "With the Civil War, a whole way of life was lost, and the southern male was emasculated. Then you come on forward through the Depression and the image of the poor white trash. Uneducated. No teeth. All that stuff. The whole South was caricatured that way, and this inferiority complex had developed after the war. So for all these years, there was this animosity building: How are we ever going to get even?"

Curry said the turning point was clear: Bear Bryant's dominance at Alabama. Fans across the region couldn't help but utter a "Roll tide!" as 'Bama emerged victorious from Los Angeles, Seattle, Happy Valley, East Rutherford, College Park, and other faraway destinations.

"It rallied something in the southern male," Curry said. "And it lasts to this day."

This book contains stories and images from some of the greatest games in college football history. It doubles as a document of southern achievement. The most successful football conference in America was dominant long before Bear Bryant, and is expected to tower over its competition for years to come.

As renowned *Sports Illustrated* writer Frank Deford wrote in a 1981 profile of Bryant, "Understand: football isn't merely popular in the South—football is Southern."

1910 VANDERBILT @ YALE

Southern schools patiently waited for their chance to learn the game of "foot ball." It was not until 1892—more than two decades after Rutgers and Princeton played the first-ever intercollegiate contest—that Georgia and A&M College of Alabama (later renamed "Auburn") met at Atlanta's Piedmont Park to begin what is now known as the Deep South's Oldest Rivalry.

A couple more decades would pass before southern football captured the nation's attention. In 1910 legendary Vanderbilt coach Dan McGugin brought his team north to New Haven, Connecticut, to face defending

1910 — Yale Tied at New Haven, 0-0

1910	
Vanderbilt	Opponents
34—Mooney	0
23—Rose Polytechnic	0
14—Castle Heights	0
18—Tennessee	0
0—Ya e	0
9—Mississippi	2
22—Louisiana State	0
23—Georgia Tech	0
23—Sewanee	6
166	8

★

1910 SQUAD

Ends: Willis T. "Slick" Stewart, Enoch "Nuck" Brown, Allen Brown, Leonard Darnell, Cecil B. Covington, J. M. "Tubby" Anderson.

Tackles: Tom Brown, Ewing Y. "Big 'Un" Freeland, Charles "Jelly" Bell.

Guards: W. E. "Frog" Metzger, George W. "Babe" Steagall, Oscar F. "Hoss" Noel, Charles H. Brown, Robert R. Brown, Wilson F. "Babe" Murrah, Frank Ridgeway.

Centers: Hugh "Buddy" Morgan, E. B. "Ted" Ross.

Quarterback: Ray Morrison.

Halfbacks: W. D. "Bill" Neely (captain), Kent Morrison, Herbert Jones, Allen B. Clark, Jr., Douglas "Duck" Henry.

Fullbacks: Henry "Bo" Williams, Carl "Zeke" Martin.

Manager: N. Baxter Jackson.

Coach: Dan E. McGugin (Michigan).

Assistants: J. N. "Stein" Stone, Bob Blake.

Front row, left to right: Fred "Rabbi" Robbins, E. B. "Ted" Ross, William E. "Frog" Metzger, Willis T. "Slick" Stewart, Cecil Covington, George W. "Babe" Steagall, Ewing Y. "Big 'Un" Freeland, Ray Morrison, Capt. Bill Neely, Henry "Bo" Williams, Oscar F. "Hoss" Noel, Frank "Tootsie" Gilliland, assistant manager, and behind him, also in street clothes, Bruce McGehee. **Middle row:** Allen Clark, Wilson Collins, Coach Dan E. McGugin, Carl T. "Zeke" Martin. Next man unidentified, J. O. Bomer, Norris Ewing, N. Baxter Jackson, manager; J. H. "Tubby" Anderson, Kent Morrison. **Top row:** W. F. "Babe" Murrah, Hugh "Buddy" Morgan, Assistant Coach Bob Blake, Dick Graham, Vance Turner, Herbert Jones, Tom Brown, Billy Howe, Ed Filbeck, Marion Adams, Douglas "Duck" Henry, Clarence Lebeck, Frank "Moose" Ridgeway, Bill Covington, Bruce Wade, Reeves, Joel B. Covington, Dan Howell, Roger Black, Charlie Brown, Enoch "Nuck" Brown.

Vanderbilt's 1910 football team was the first southern opponent to face mighty Yale on the gridiron. The teams tied 0–0, and the surprising result was enough to inspire a late-night parade through Nashville.

VANDERBILT UNIVERSITY SPECIAL COLLECTIONS AND UNIVERSITY ARCHIVES

national champion Yale. The Commodores managed to stifle the powerful Bulldogs for a 0–0 tie.

"The field was slippery and the ball heavy," reported the *Wilmington Morning Star*, but "the visitors knew football and the 11 worked with machine like precision and aggressively from the start."

Yale, playing a southern team for the first time in its history, had the ball at Vanderbilt's 10-yard line on three occasions but failed to cross the goal line.

"It was easy enough to see at the start that the southerners had made up their minds to give Yale a fight to remember, whoever won," the *Nashville Tennessean* reported.

Nobody technically emerged victorious, but you wouldn't know it from the [*Tennessean*]'s tone: "With Dan McGugin at the helm, they have all shown the eastern wing of the continent that football is gradually obtaining a foothold in the south . . . Considering the odds he faced, the Commodore wizard has achieved the finest victory of his great career."

In celebration, a group of more than 1,000 male students paraded through the streets of Nashville wearing "nightshirts, pajamas and curtailed bonnets." Stops included Belmont (still a women-only college) for a late-night serenade and Vanderbilt's Dudley Field for a bonfire that lasted "until far past the hour for young persons of tender years to be up."

1917 PENN @ GEORGIA TECH

Coached by John Heisman—yes, that Heisman—Tech entered this marquee matchup having gone undefeated for nearly three years. The previous season, Heisman's team had handed down the ugliest score in college football history: a 222–0 whipping of Cumberland.

Despite that success, the Engineers were not an easy pick to beat Penn, Heisman's alma mater. The visiting Quakers—making their first trip to the South—had earned a Rose Bowl bid the season prior, and had just blown out Albright College by 63 points a few days before traveling to Atlanta.

It didn't take long for Penn to realize it was outmatched both physically and strategically.

Heisman's innovative "jump shift" offense featured a column of three Engineers backs that would shift in unison just before the snap to overload one side of the formation. This allowed Tech a major advantage as it bulldozed past defenses.

In the days before film existed, the Quakers could only imagine what the famous "jump shift" would look like. Whatever pregame visualization they tried didn't work. Tech running back Everett Strupper ran for a 70-yard touchdown early in the game, and the 41–0 rout was on. Heisman's team finished the season 9–0 while outscoring its opponents 491–17 (that's not a typo) to earn the South's first national title.

1926 ROSE BOWL: ALABAMA VS. WASHINGTON ("THE GAME THAT CHANGED THE SOUTH")

The afterglow of Alabama's watershed 1922 win over Penn—a 9–7 victory that shocked Grantland Rice and the rest of the East Coast media and thrust the Crimson Tide into the national spotlight for the first time—was cut tragically short for coach Xen C. Scott, who was secretly suffering from throat cancer and was forced to step down soon after the season.

Alabama was not the Rose Bowl's first choice (or second or third), but the Crimson Tide pulled off a 20–19 upset of Washington dubbed "The Game That Changed the South."
WIKIMEDIA COMMONS

While searching for a replacement, the university first asked Vanderbilt's Dan McGugin to come to Tuscaloosa, but the Commodores legend declined. Instead, he told the Crimson Tide to pursue Vandy assistant Wallace Wade. The subsequent hire changed college football and established Alabama as much more than a one-hit wonder.

Wade's 1925 team went 9–0 during the regular season while allowing just one touchdown. However, that supreme show of force was not enough to catch the attention of the Rose Bowl, which was college football's only bowl game at the time. "The Granddaddy of Them All" invited four other schools, including fellow Southern Conference member Tulane. Each one declined, forcing the Rose Bowl committee to extend an invitation to the Crimson Tide.

Alabama's opponent would be mighty Washington, which featured All-American running back Georgia "Wildcat" Wilson and a group of massive linemen. Unsurprisingly, West Coast media outlets were certain of a Huskies victory. Washington was installed as a 2-to-1 favorite.

The Huskies built a 12–0 halftime lead thanks in part to a touchdown and interception by Wilson, and Alabama appeared outmatched in the biggest game of the season.

Many years later, Alabama fullback Grant Gillis recounted coach Wade's halftime speech to the *Birmingham News*: "We were dejected country boys, had our lip out. Wade came in late after everybody was sitting down. He said 'and they told me that boys from the South would fight.' And he walked out. That's all he said."

The third quarter belonged to 'Bama. Wade's team scored three touchdowns in a span of seven minutes, with the go-ahead touchdown coming on a 30-yard touchdown pass from Allison "Pooley" Hubert to Johnny Mack Brown (a running back who used his stellar Rose Bowl performance to kickstart a Hollywood acting career that lasted nearly five decades).

Washington scored once more to close the gap to 20–19, but Alabama held strong to capture the upset.

The *Birmingham News* likened the shock to a tidal wave brought about by a "vicious tornado." Alabama celebrated all the way back to Tuscaloosa, stopping its passenger train in various cities along the way to receive cheers and gifts.

That "vicious tornado" stirred up change in Pasadena; 13 more southern teams were invited to the Rose Bowl before the event entered into an exclusive Pacific–Big Ten partnership in 1946.

To this day, Alabama's 1926 victory lives on in the school's fight song, which concludes with the following lyrics: "Fight on, fight on, fight on, men! Remember the Rose Bowl we'll win then! Go, roll to victory, Hit your stride, You're Dixie's football pride, Crimson Tide!"

1939 ORANGE BOWL: TENNESSEE VS. OKLAHOMA

Earnie Seiler was tired of running a second-rate postseason game. In four years, he had only managed to convince one ranked team—Duquesne— to show up in Miami for the Orange Bowl.

In 1939 Seiler decided to go the extra mile (or 1,500). He wanted the undefeated, No. 2-ranked Oklahoma Sooners to play in Miami, so he visited Norman with a "persuasion kit" in tow. The Sugar and Cotton Bowls were also in town—and they were offering twice as much money—but Seiler had a leg up, so to speak.

"When I came in, the Sugar and Cotton people didn't even give me a second look," Seiler said decades later. "They weren't worried a bit. Then I brought out my pictures: palm trees, beaches, blue Atlantic Ocean. But especially the girls. I wasn't so dumb that I didn't remember what I used to play for. 'Would you rather go to Dallas?' I said. 'Come to Miami. We'll have ourselves a party.'"

The players loved it, and the administration was similarly smitten. At Seiler's urging, the Oklahoma president made a phone call to the University of Tennessee, and the Orange Bowl quickly had a titanic matchup on its hands.

The SEC was still a new entity at that point; its charter members had seceded from the Southern Conference in 1932. And while Alabama won the green conference's first national title in 1934, no SEC team had since been able to follow the Tide to the top.

That ended in the 1938 season, when Robert Neyland's Volunteers emerged from a three-year hibernation to ignite one of the most impressive streaks in college football history. Backfield stars George Cafego and Babe Wood highlighted a stellar offense, but it was Neyland's suffocating defense that would be remembered as the championship catalyst.

Neyland, a pioneer in film study, had engineered four consecutive shutouts entering the Orange Bowl, and his Vols extended that streak with a convincing—and notably physical—17–0 win over the Sooners.

"Miami dentists should do a land office business tomorrow building false teeth," wrote Scoop Latimer of the *Greenville News*, "while orthopedic surgeons might have their hands full repairing cracked ribs."

Bloody faces and all, Tennessee outgained Oklahoma on the ground, 203–23, to earn the school's first national title.

The Volunteers quickly became the most feared program in the country, pitching 15 consecutive shutouts before surrendering another point.

In Neyland's final 33 games before he left to fight in World War II, his defense surrendered an impossibly low 2 points per contest.

To the glee of Seiler, the Orange Bowl executive, Tennessee's heavyweight win over Oklahoma also created a celebrated college football tradition. Sportswriters from New York, Washington, Chicago, and dozens of other cities had witnessed the spectacle and wanted more.

The consensus, per the *Greenville News*: "The splendor of this setting eclipsed all football classics."

1962 SUGAR BOWL: ALABAMA VS. ARKANSAS

When Bear Bryant arrived at the University of Alabama in 1958, the SEC was in the midst of a tremendous power display. Tennessee (1950 and 1951), Georgia Tech (1952), and Auburn (1957) had already collected national titles, and three more would come in quick succession from LSU (1958) and Ole Miss (1959 and 1960).

Alabama, once the pride of the conference, had suffered four consecutive losing seasons, including an embarrassing 0–10 record in 1955.

Bryant swiftly rebuilt. By his fourth season, the Crimson Tide had achieved the inverse of its lowest moment by stringing together a 10–0 regular season. Entering its Sugar Bowl matchup, Alabama was the consensus national champion and had a chance to finish undefeated for the first time in 16 years.

The roadblock: No. 9-ranked Arkansas, which was riding a five-game winning streak and had just secured its third consecutive Southwest Conference title. Coach Frank Broyles and running back Lance Alworth were on their way to Hall of Fame careers, and—late in the second half of the Sugar Bowl—the Razorbacks had reason to believe they could pull the upset.

Trailing 10–3, Arkansas quarterback George McKinney hit Alworth for a 31-yard gain into Alabama territory, but Alworth fumbled the ball away. On a subsequent drive, McKinney tossed another 37-yard completion to the Alabama 40-yard line, and then narrowly missed Alworth in the end zone for what would have been the tying touchdown.

Bryant estimated he suffered "nine heart attacks" throughout the contest, with the majority likely coming on Arkansas's final drive.

But Alabama defender Butch Wilson ended the Hogs' threat with an interception inches in front of the goal line. 'Bama completed its undefeated championship season, and would go on to dominate the SEC picture for two more decades until Bryant's death in 1983.

1967 OLE MISS @ KENTUCKY

There's a famous story about SEC integration that features (who else?) Bear Bryant. It is widely believed that he scheduled a 1970 game vs. powerhouse Southern Cal—a team with several prominent African-American players—in hopes it would convince Alabama governor George Wallace and the rest of the state's hard-stance football fans to change their minds about black football players.

Led by Sam "Bam" Cunningham, No. 1 USC arrived in Birmingham that autumn and shredded the Crimson Tide by three touchdowns. It was the second time in as many years the Alabama faithful had seen its

Kentucky captain Wilbur Hackett (41) helped break down the SEC color barrier after teammate Nate Northington (23) became the first African-American player in conference history.
UNIVERSITY OF KENTUCKY LIBRARY SPECIAL COLLECTIONS RESEARCH CENTER

all-white team blown over by African-American athletes. (A 41–14 loss to Tennessee the year before featured black receiver Lester McClain and black linebacker Jackie Walker. The game was termed "A NIGHTMARE IN BRIGHT DAYLIGHT" by the *Tuscaloosa News*.)

Cunningham remembered the eerie silence of Legion Field, no jeers or racial epithets. Just the realization that change was coming.

"Basically what they were witnessing was the future because they saw what their program was going to be in the years to come," Cunningham said in 2016. "So as shocked as they might've been at the time, I'm sure they've come to appreciate what happened that evening. Because it benefited the University of Alabama and teams in the SEC much more than it benefited us."

Backup USC quarterback Craig Fertig told reporter Allen Barra that he witnessed a peculiar moment in the postgame scrum.

"I swear, Coach Bryant had a smile on his face," Fertig said. "His team had just gotten whipped by three touchdowns, and here's the man who [USC coach] John McKay had always told me hated to lose more than any man on Earth, and he's smiling. I'll never forget what he said. He said, 'John, I can't thank you enough.'"

The Crimson Tide integrated its varsity roster the following season (black freshman Wilbur Jackson was already on campus in 1970), and Bryant won three more national titles within a decade.

Some still question whether Bryant was making a political statement, but Sylvester Croom—a 1971 recruit and the SEC's first black head coach—is part of a larger contingent that gives the 'Bama legend credit for easing a change-resistant fanbase into the future.

"My feeling was that he waited until he thought the time was right," Croom said in 2004. "I really believe that game with Southern Cal was an instrument in the plan of getting that done. He knew Southern Cal had black players. The unique thing to me was he scheduled that first game in Alabama. There's no question in my mind that was not an accident."

Alabama was late to integration, even by SEC standards.

Nearly 500 miles to the North, the University of Kentucky football program recruited a pair of African-American players in late 1965: Nate

Northington and Greg Page. Kentucky governor Ned Breathitt was so intent on seeing a black Wildcats athlete that he personally hosted Northington at the governor's mansion during the Louisville athlete's recruitment.

Northington agreed to play after that grand gesture. Page—a Middlesboro native who had marched with Martin Luther King Jr.—followed. The former became the first black man to compete in a varsity athletics contest for a member of the Southeastern Conference on September 30, 1967.

The latter died the night before.

Rewind to August of that year: Northington and Page had already completed a season on the Kentucky freshman squad. Their first varsity action was approaching, and the Wildcats were running a simple pursuit drill in practice. The defense's goal: to converge upon the ball carrier as he ran down the sideline.

Per the reporting of SEC Country's Joe Mussatto, Page was first to reach the runner, but another teammate crashed into him from behind. He crumpled to the ground, paralyzed from the neck down. Page spent 38 days in the hospital until he passed away. Northington, a frequent visitor to Page's bedside, would become the first black man to play in the SEC fewer than 24 hours after his roommate's death.

He officially played 3 minutes, 17 seconds before leaving the game with a shoulder injury. The Associated Press game story made no mention of Northington's accomplishment. In the following weeks, he served as pallbearer at Page's funeral and slowly slipped out of the picture in Lexington.

After coaches took away his meal ticket for missing too many classes (many during Page's hospitalization), Northington approached the only other black players on the team—freshmen Wilbur Hackett and Houston Hogg—and told them to finish what he and Page had started.

"I had had enough," Northington said of his decision to transfer to Western Kentucky. "And I couldn't take any more."

His contribution was more than enough to hasten change. Hackett would soon become the SEC's first black captain, and more than half of the conference's schools landed a black football recruit before the end of the 1960s.

FIRST AFRICAN-AMERICAN FOOTBALL PLAYERS FOR EACH SEC SCHOOL

From left: Mel Page (representing his father, Greg), Nate Northington, Wilbur Hackett and Houston Hogg. Kentucky installed a statue to honor the four players in 2016.

MARK CORNELISON/*LEXINGTON HERALD-LEADER* VIA AP

Alabama in 1971: **John Mitchell** (Mobile, Alabama)—A junior-college transfer who went on to become the school's first black assistant coach and later the SEC's first black coordinator, at LSU in 1990. **Wilbur Jackson** (Ozark, Alabama)—The Crimson Tide's first black football signee, in 1970. He was selected No. 9 overall by the San Francisco 49ers in the 1974 NFL Draft and won a Super Bowl ring with the Washington Redskins.

    Auburn in 1969: **James Owens** (Fairfield, Alabama)—He scored five touchdowns during his Auburn career. "I realized, it's no longer about you," he said in 2012. "It's about all these that are believing in you, hoping in you."

Florida in 1970: **Willie Jackson** (Sarasota, Florida)—A three-year starter at receiver. "We wanted to show them we were just like anybody else, and we had the ability to compete in the classroom," he said in 1991. **Leonard George** (Tampa, Florida)—First black scholarship player at Florida, one day ahead of Jackson in December 1968. The running back scored his lone career touchdown at Alabama in 1970 before moving to defensive back as a junior and senior.

Georgia in 1972: **Horace King** (Athens, Georgia)—The football star of the group, he scored 19 career touchdowns and was named All-SEC before an eight-year NFL career with the Detroit Lions. He originally planned to attend Michigan State, but stayed home so his mother could see him play. **Richard Appleby** (Athens, Georgia)—Famous in Athens for an 80-yard trick-play touchdown pass to beat Florida in 1975. **Clarence Pope** (Athens, Georgia)—Transferred following the 1974 season. He recalled upperclassmen dressing as Ku Klux Klan members and brandishing shotguns during his first day on campus. **Chuck Kinnebrew** (Rome, Georgia)—An all-state football star and state champion in wrestling and discus as a prep, he eventually made the starting lineup as a defensive tackle. **Larry West** (Albany, Georgia)—A four-year letterman at defensive back, he was inducted into the Albany Sports Hall of Fame in 1990.

Kentucky in 1967: **Nate Northington** (Louisville, Kentucky)—First SEC athlete to compete in a varsity contest, playing 3 minutes, 17 seconds at Ole Miss. Transferred to Western Kentucky during his sophomore year. **Greg Page** (Middlesboro, Kentucky)—Arrived in 1966 with Northington, but was paralyzed during a drill before his sophomore season and died the night before Northington broke the color barrier. **Wilbur Hackett** (Louisville, Kentucky)—First black team captain in SEC history. After completing his career in 1971, he said he was harassed by Mississippi state police before a game vs. Ole Miss, as well as forced out of a Baton Rouge, Louisiana, restaurant. **Houston Hogg** (Owensboro, Kentucky)—A running back, he experienced white teammates purposely missing blocks on the field and excluding him socially off it. Of his opponents, he said, "Something could happen out there on the field, and you just prayed it wouldn't happen to you. In college, they showed no mercy."

LSU in 1972: **Mikell Williams** (New Orleans, Louisiana)—Started every game as a sophomore cornerback. He eventually earned All-America honors and then intercepted 24 passes for the NFL's San Diego Chargers and Los Angeles Rams. **Lora O. Hinton** (Chesapeake, Virginia)—The first black student at Great Bridge High School injured his knee as a college freshman, forcing him to delay his varsity debut from '72 to '73. He finished his career with 396 rushing yards and two touchdowns.

Mississippi in 1973: **Robert Williams** (Yazoo City, Mississippi)—Nick-named "Gentle Ben," he became an All-America offensive lineman and played 10 seasons for the NFL's Buffalo Bills. He also wrestled a bear at halftime at an Ole Miss basketball game. **James Reed** (Meridian, Missis-sippi)—An All-SEC running back, he later served as a special agent for the famed Naval Criminal Investigative Service.

Mississippi State in 1970: **Robert Bell** (Meridian, Mississippi)—Played defensive tackle for three seasons and graduated with a degree in business administration. "I haven't really talked about the bad times," he said in 2004. "I kind of buried them and let them lay." **Frank Dowsing** (Tupelo, Mississippi)—He helped integrate the local high school in Tupelo before earning All-America honors as a Bulldogs defensive back.

Tennessee in 1968: **Lester McClain** (Antioch, Tennessee)—In '67 he became the first African-American athlete to sign a scholarship with Ten-nessee. He recorded 1,003 receiving yards and 10 touchdowns. **Jackie Walker** (Knoxville, Tennessee)—Saw his first varsity action in '69 and eventually became Tennessee's first black team captain. With five career interception returns for touchdowns, he's still tied for the most in NCAA history.

Vanderbilt in 1971: **Taylor Stokes** (Clarksville, Tennessee)—As a sophomore, went 15-for-15 on extra-point attempts and kicked a game-winning 40-yard field goal vs. Tampa. He withdrew from Vandy follow-ing his junior season for a combination of academic, social, and family reasons. **James Hurley** (Atlanta, Georgia)—Transferred from Georgia to Vanderbilt as a walk-on in 1970. He lettered, but it's unclear if he saw any playing time. **Walter Overton** (Nashville, Tennessee)—Followed Stokes as the second African American to sign with Vandy out of high school. The quarterback-turned-receiver earned All-SEC honors and is now the general manager of Nissan Stadium, home of the Tennessee Titans.

"Besides my family, the only reason I picked [Kentucky] was because of Nat and Greg," Hackett said in 2013. "They told us we had an opportunity to do a good thing, turn the football program around, and in doing that open doors for African-American athletes."

1980 GEORGIA @ TENNESSEE

One year after ESPN aired its first episode of *SportsCenter*, the SEC provided a superstar for cable subscribers across the country.

Herschel Walker, an 18-year-old from Wrightsville, Georgia, was a fourth-string running back for the Bulldogs when they traveled to Knoxville on September 6, 1980. More than 95,000 fans—at the time, the largest football crowd the South had ever seen—packed into Neyland Stadium to greet the No. 16-ranked team in the country.

Georgia was punchless as Tennessee built up a 9–0 halftime lead. Walker had seen a couple series but hadn't done anything of note. When he first found out he was going into the game, he couldn't even find his helmet.

The coaching staff decided to make a change during the break: Walker would start the second half and stay in the game, for better or worse.

It got worse . . . for Tennessee.

Facing a 15–2 deficit with the ball at the Tennessee 16-yard line, Walker took a handoff and slipped through the right side of the line. He cut back and found one man standing between him and the end zone: Volunteers safety Bill Bates.

Bates, a future three-time Super Bowl champion with the Dallas Cowboys, became a human turnstile as Walker smashed him to the turf, then stomped over him for a game-changing score.

"I looked into Herschel's eyes and realized he wasn't going to make a move," Bates said more than three decades later. "The next thing I knew, I had footprints on my chest and saw No. 34 running into the end zone for a touchdown."

In his radio call, Georgia play-by-play man Larry Munson let loose one of his most famous lines: "My God, a freshman!"

Walker scored again in the fourth quarter, and Georgia escaped, 16–15. The Bulldogs used that SEC opener as fuel for a 12-game winning

Herschel Walker was a fourth-string Georgia running back when the Bulldogs arrived in Knoxville on Sept. 6, 1980. Three hours later, he was a star.
AP PHOTO

streak that propelled them all the way to the Sugar Bowl. Walker was outstanding in a win vs. Notre Dame (150 yards, 2 touchdowns), and Georgia secured its most recent national title.

"That running back is something God puts on this earth every several decades or so," Tennessee coach Johnny Majors said after losing to Georgia by 44 points in 1981. "He has more power, speed, and strength than anyone I've ever seen. He's got more going for him than any player that's ever played this game."

To list all of his accomplishments would require a separate book, but the SEC's all-time leading rusher kicked off a decade that would also feature legendary Auburn running back Bo Jackson. Each man won a Heisman Trophy (Walker in '82, Jackson in '85) as the conference shifted out of the Bryant era.

1992 SEC CHAMPIONSHIP GAME: ALABAMA VS. FLORIDA

It was plain: a conference championship game would hurt—not help—the Southeastern Conference. Imagine a top-ranked SEC team blowing its shot at a national title thanks to an upset by some plucky rival in early December. A nightmare!

Commissioner Roy Kramer's proposal made coaches sick.

"They were convinced this was the end of the SEC," Kramer said hours before the 25th edition of the game he created. "We would never have another national championship."

Kramer didn't listen to his coaches; he didn't even call the NCAA for approval (though he did have an attorney double-check the rulebook).

In 1990 his conference was in uncharted territory, and he was ready to surprise the country. Arkansas and South Carolina had signed on in August to bring the league to 12 teams. The East and West divisions finally solidified after months of debate (Auburn wanted to play in the East; Kramer didn't want to see the Iron Bowl played in consecutive weeks).

So he pulled the trigger, and his unthinkable idea has now led to common practice. All 10 Football Bowl Subdivision conferences held championship games in 2017.

Speaking at the same 25th anniversary press conference, Florida's Steve Spurrier claimed he was one of the proponents, citing a need to move away from co-champions and have one winner standing at the end of the regular season. Alabama's Gene Stallings admitted he was not.

Alabama coach Gene Stallings was a staunch opponent of the SEC championship game. He softened his stance after Crimson Tide cornerback Antonio Langham scored the game-winning touchdown (pictured) in 1992.
AP PHOTO/CURTIS COMPTON

His Alabama team was undefeated and ranked No. 2 in December 1992. The nightmare was unfolding before the league's eyes.

"I'm 11–0 and I haven't won anything," he told Kramer in a 1992 phone call. "What the hell are we doing playing this game?"

Spurrier's Gators and Stallings's Crimson Tide met at Legion Field in Birmingham for the first edition. The college football world watched a classic unfold on ABC, as Florida rallied from a two-touchdown deficit to tie the game, 21–21, with 8:01 remaining.

Florida quarterback Shane Matthews was cooking, and the Gators defense sacked Alabama passer Jay Barker twice on the following possession.

So it was that Matthews and the UF offense got a chance to win with a little more than three minutes on the clock. The two-time SEC Player of the Year took a five-step drop and looked to the right sideline, where receiver Monty Duncan was curling.

That's when Alabama defensive back Antonio Langham earned himself a place in SEC history by stepping in front of Matthews's pass and returning it 27 yards for the game-winning touchdown.

'Bama went on to win its first national title since Bear Bryant's death, while Matthews's decorated career became shrouded by a single throw.

The Florida *Sun-Sentinel* called it "SHANE'S SHAME," saying, "In the heart of SEC country, in the land of Bear Bryant and Alabama football, Shane Matthews' most memorable touchdown pass will be the one he threw to a Crimson Tide defensive back Saturday."

ESPN later released a documentary entitled *The Play That Changed College Football*.

Whatever the name, Stallings was suddenly content with playing the extra game. And 25 years after opposing the change, he was more than willing to give Kramer credit for a monumental decision.

"I think the commissioner came up with a great idea," he admitted.

2007 BCS NATIONAL CHAMPIONSHIP GAME: FLORIDA VS. OHIO STATE

Entering the national title game in January 2007, Big Ten football was all the rage. No. 1 Ohio State and No. 2 Michigan had played their version of "the Game of the Century" a month and a half earlier, and many analysts wanted to see a rematch in the BCS championship.

Florida, the official choice to face Ohio State, was not as attractive of a draw. The Gators were a defense-oriented, run-centric SEC team that had lost to Auburn by 10 points earlier in the year and narrowly avoided defeat on a few other occasions.

Nationally, the conference reputation was down. An SEC team had appeared in only one title game over the past seven seasons, and Auburn's undefeated 2004 squad was left out of the championship game entirely.

Perhaps that's why Gators coach Urban Meyer—two years removed from a successful stint at Utah—felt the need to politic in mid-November. He irked Michigan coach Lloyd Carr by calling a potential Big Ten rematch "unfair to Ohio State," adding, "I think it'd be unfair to the country."

Do-it-all Florida athlete Percy Harvin was the perfect embodiment of the SEC's new emphasis on speed. He and the Gators raced past Ohio State in the 2007 BCS National Championship Game.
AP PHOTO/MARK J. TERRILL

The debate was controversial enough that Ohio State coach Jim Tressel elected not to submit a final regular-season ballot in the coaches' poll.

Tressel and the Buckeyes had won a national title four years prior, and his 2006 squad was supposed to be one of the best in school history. Ohio

Florida coach Urban Meyer was the architect of a Gators team that served notice to the rest of the nation: The SEC was playing a superior brand of football.
AP PHOTO/MARK J. TERRILL

State had blown out nearly every one of its opponents—including then-No. 2 Texas—before sneaking past Michigan in what was effectively the Big Ten championship game.

Quarterback Troy Smith (30 touchdown passes against five interceptions) won the Heisman Trophy in a landslide, and he had a pair of receivers, Ted Ginn Jr. and Anthony Gonzalez, who would become first-round draft picks the following spring.

Ginn Jr. seemingly showed why Ohio State was a 7-point favorite when he returned the Gators' opening kickoff for a 93-yard touchdown.

Then, the party was over.

The speedster hurt his foot while celebrating the score and hobbled off the field after Ohio State's first offensive play. By the time he returned to the sideline—with crutches—Florida was winning by 20 points.

Meyer's defense had made Smith's life hell. The Heisman winner had no room to throw or escape as the Gators' pass-rushers consistently broke free in the backfield. He finished with just four completions for 35 yards and an interception. His rushing total (including sacks) was minus-29.

"Troy, I've never met a Heisman Trophy winner before," linebacker Brian Crum reportedly shouted at Smith, who was lying on the turf with the football nearby after a second-quarter sack. "I mean, except maybe Danny Wuerffel. So, Troy, would you please sign that ball?"

On the other side, OSU had no answers for Florida's speed. Senior quarterback Chris Leak finished 25-of-35 for 213 yards, while freshman backup Tim Tebow rushed 10 times for 39 yards and completed a "jump" pass to close out a shocking 41–14 victory.

Florida's second-ever national title would be the first of seven consecutive championships for the Southeastern Conference from 2006 to 2012. That span would include rings for LSU and Auburn, as well as launch what is now one of the greatest dynasties in college football history. (Don't worry, Alabama fans; we'll get there.)

If the writing wasn't on the wall for the Big Ten and other leagues around the country, Gators lineman Jarvin Moss made it clear in a postgame interview.

"Honestly, we've played a lot better teams than them," Moss said. "I could name four or five teams in the SEC that could probably compete with them and play the same type of game we did."

PART 2:
THE IRON BOWL

Per the *Birmingham News*, 450 people were in attendance at a Birmingham baseball field in late February 1893 to witness a 32–22 Auburn victory over Alabama. It was the first time the University of Alabama had competed against Auburn University in the new sport, and the contest would engender a 12-game series between the rivals over 15 years.

Accounts differ on what forced the teams apart from 1908 to 1948. Was it a series of overly physical games in the early years? A disdain for the brutish gridiron's growing popularity?

The boring answer is hotel compensation. Per the *News*, Alabama and Auburn coaches could not agree upon the rate at which its players would stay in Birmingham for the 1908 game. Thus, a difference of $34 was the reason for a four-decades-long break in the action between the Tigers and Crimson Tide.

When the schools finally met again in 1948, it was a figurative bloodbath. Alabama smacked Auburn, 55–0, at Birmingham's Legion Field, and the teams reignited a rivalry that is now arguably the country's best.

The first modern Alabama-Auburn classic arrived in 1964. Though the term "Iron Bowl" had been thrown around during the 1950s, legendary Auburn coach Shug Jordan solidified the phrase in college football lore during the week leading up to the '64 edition. Asked whether he was disappointed that his underachieving Tigers would not reach the postseason that year, Jordan responded, "We've got our bowl game. We have it every year. It's the Iron Bowl in Birmingham."

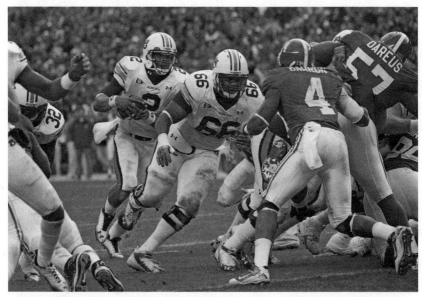

The Iron Bowl rivalry between Alabama and Auburn kicked off in 1893 and continues to fuel debate in the Yellowhammer State. Pictured: Auburn quarterback Cam Newton leads an unforgettable "Camback" against 'Bama in 2010.
AP PHOTO/BUTCH DILL

(Important context: Birmingham was once the largest iron and steel producer in the country.)

It was the first nationally televised game between Alabama and Auburn, and the teams put on a show for NBC viewers.

Underdog Auburn had a narrow 7–6 advantage out of the halftime break. It didn't last long. Crimson Tide return man Ray Ogden fielded the opening kickoff 7 yards deep in his own end zone, and—in a decision that fooled both his opponents and his own blockers—brought it out for a 107-yard touchdown return.

Quarterback Joe Namath hit Ray Perkins for a 23-yard fourth-quarter touchdown that served as the winning score in a 21–14 victory. In those days the national title was awarded before bowl season, so the win gave Bear Bryant's Crimson Tide a championship (Alabama subsequently lost to Texas in the Cotton Bowl, but it still claims the 1964 title).

That game served as the introduction to the Iron Bowl's modern era, and fans still remember the best games by their monikers: "the Run in the Mud," "Punt Bama Punt" and "the Kick Six."

In recent years these programs have only gotten stronger. Auburn went undefeated in 2004, won the 2010 national title, and made another title-game appearance following the 2013 season. Alabama's run of five national titles under Nick Saban has been nothing short of legendary. At the end of each regular season, the nation's eyes have been on the Iron Bowl, and why not? The rivalry has featured a No. 1 or No. 2 team in each of the past 10 contests.

1967 IRON BOWL ("THE RUN IN THE MUD")

On the morning of December 3, 1967, Charles Land's lede for the *Tuscaloosa News* was as follows: "Maybe Alabama football coach Paul William Bryant can't really walk on the water. Maybe Alabama quarterback Kenny (Snake) Stabler can't, either. But Stabler can run on it."

Ken Stabler, future Pro Football Hall of Fame quarterback and Super Bowl champion with the Oakland Raiders, had his best years ahead of him. But the most famous play of his career? That had happened the night before in Birmingham.

No. 8 Alabama met unranked Auburn in the Magic City with a three-game Iron Bowl winning streak in tow. Stabler was one of the SEC's best passers, but a monsoon turned Legion Field into a cesspool. Auburn dominated much of a sloppy game, eventually converting its field position into a 38-yard field goal.

That 3–0 deficit might as well have been 30–0 for Stabler and the Crimson Tide. On the game broadcast, the muddy field appeared to be made of shimmering molten lava.

It was, then, with great difficulty that Stabler rolled around the right side of the Alabama line and—deciding he could not pitch the ball to his option back—began the slowest 47-yard touchdown run in history.

With mud serving as a speed equalizer, Stabler evaded his Auburn pursuers and crashed into the end zone as a defensive back finally made contact.

In 2015 "the Snake" passed away at 69 years of age. His on-field legacy was rock solid: a national championship ring in 1965 (as a backup). An undefeated season in '66. The NFL's MVP award in '74. A Super Bowl ring in '76. A spot on the NFL's 1970s All-Decade team. Induction into several halls of fame. The list goes on.

But one moment stood out from all the others.

In the words of the *News*'s Paul Davis after the 1967 Iron Bowl: "Countless tornadoes touched down in Mississippi and several Alabama towns. Then one named Stabler skipped through the north end of Legion Field."

1972 IRON BOWL ("PUNT BAMA PUNT")

Millennial SEC fans have "the Kick Six." Their parents and grandparents have "Punt Bama Punt."

The key word when retelling the unbelievable fourth quarter of Auburn's 1972 win over Alabama is "AGAIN." As in: "Bill Newton blocked an Alabama punt, and David Langner ran it back for a touchdown. Then, they did it AGAIN."

The scene: Undefeated, No. 2-ranked Alabama was well on its way to victory vs. the overachieving "Amazins" of Auburn. The Crimson Tide led 16–0 with about 10 minutes remaining when Auburn finally got on the scoreboard with a field goal.

"Everybody in the stadium Legion Field in Birmingham—35,000 on one side wearing red, 35,000 on the other wearing orange and blue—got up and booed [Auburn coach] Shug [Jordan] for kicking the field goal," Alabama assistant Pat Dye later told ESPN. "Our fans were booing because he'd spoiled the shutout, and their fans were booing because they thought he'd given up."

Alabama was content to run clock and bleed out the Tigers with an elite defense. Problem was, 'Bama couldn't even get its defense on the field. With nearly six minutes remaining, Auburn's Newton blocked a Greg Gantt punt. Langner, a Tigers defensive back, scooped it up and ran it back for a surprising touchdown.

Surprise quickly became shock when Alabama was forced to punt once more, and Auburn repeated its trick: Newton blocked it. Langner

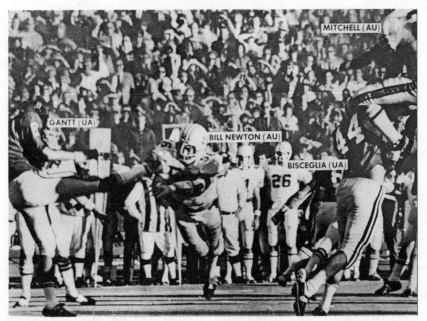

Alabama punter Greg Gantt and blocker Steve Bisceglia fail to prevent Auburn's Bill Newton and David Langner from pulling off an unbelievable sequence of special-teams heroics.
HAYWOOD PARAVICINI/AL.COM VIA AP

scooped it up and ran it back. After the extra point, Auburn held an impossible 17–16 lead with 1:34 to go.

Langner, a soft-spoken junior from Birmingham, also intercepted the Crimson Tide's first and last passes of the day. Afterward, he sat quietly near his locker, holding a pair of footballs as his teammates turned the room into a madhouse.

"It was just unbelievable for this to happen," Langner said. "The greatest game. The greatest moment of my life."

In the years before YouTube reaction videos, fans' grief was typically recorded in print. Alabama's 1973 yearbook, the *Corolla*, provided the following synopsis:

Ala 16.

Aub 3.

Santa Claus 14.

1981 IRON BOWL

Bear Bryant's big day appeared to be ruined, and one of his pupils was to blame.

Former Alabama assistant and first-year Auburn coach Pat Dye had his unranked Tigers up on the No. 4 Crimson Tide, 17–14, with 12:58 remaining. If the Tigers prevailed, Bryant would need to wait a month for another chance to break Amos Alonzo Stagg's record for all-time victories.

His players apparently were tired of hearing about the record, so they took action at Legion Field. Crimson Tide quarterback Walter Lewis— the third 'Bama passer under center that day—found Jesse Bendross for a 38-yard go-ahead touchdown. On the next drive, running back Linnie Patrick unleashed a pair of dazzling runs to make it 28–17.

Win No. 315 was in the books. The Bear's to-do list was officially complete. His legacy was set. In fact, Alabama had already renamed its coliseum to Bryant-Denny Stadium two years prior.

"When I first came here I was fightin' for my life out there on the field," Bryant told *Sports Illustrated* the summer before that 1981 season. "Well, I'm still fightin' for my life. It's just that I don't have near as many years left."

Following his record-breaking win, the Bear coached one more season at Alabama. He ran his career record to 323–85–17 and beat Illinois in the Liberty Bowl before retiring from football. On January 23, 1983, Paul William Bryant suffered a fatal heart attack.

Per the *Birmingham News*, on the day of Bryant's funeral, an estimated 250,000 mourners lined the 60-mile path between Tuscaloosa and his burial place in Birmingham.

"I think Coach Bryant was the greatest leader this country ever had," former Alabama star and then-Dallas Cowboys linebacker Lee Roy Jordan said at the cemetery. "And not just the leader of Alabama football players, but of the whole nation."

1982 IRON BOWL ("BO OVER THE TOP")

There is no better SEC debate than Herschel Walker vs. Bo Jackson. The larger-than-life running backs each won a Heisman Trophy during the 1980s, and both began dominating the conference as freshmen. Walker's

Auburn freshman Bo Jackson spoils Bear Bryant's final game against the Tigers with a 4th-and-goal leap in 1982. "He got in on that last wiggle," noted Auburn coach Pat Dye. AP PHOTO

ALL-TIME WINNINGEST SEC COACHES

Alabama players carry coach Bear Bryant off the field after a 35–0 victory over Auburn in 1973. The win was one of Bryant's 292 as an SEC coach. AP PHOTO

Since his record-breaking victory in 1981, Bear Bryant has been bumped down to third all-time behind Penn State's Joe Paterno (409 wins) and Florida State's Bobby Bowden (357). The Bear can take solace in his spot atop the SEC leaderboard, which should be safe for a long, long time.

Here's a list of the most wins by a coach while working an SEC side-line (Bryant's time at Texas A&M does not count, nor does Saban's time at Michigan State; both conference and nonconference games included; SIAC and Southern contests do not count):

1. Bear Bryant, Kentucky/Alabama (1946–1953, 1958–1982):   292–69–15

2. Steve Spurrier, Florida/South Carolina (1990–2001, 2005–2015):   208–76–1

3. Vince Dooley, Georgia (1964–1988):   201–77–10

4. John Vaught, Ole Miss (1947–1970, 1973):   190–61–12

5. (tie) Nick Saban, LSU/Alabama (2000–2004, 2007–present):   175–36

6. (tie) Ralph Jordan, Auburn (1951–1975):   175–83–7

7. Phillip Fulmer, Tennessee (1992–2008):   152–52

8. Mark Richt, Georgia (2001–2015):   145–51

9. Bobby Dodd, Georgia Tech (1945–1963):   142–56–7

10. Wally Butts, Georgia (1939–1960):   140–86–9

11. Charles McClendon, LSU (1962–1979):   137–59–7

12. Johnny Majors, Tennessee (1977–1992):   116–62–8

13. Les Miles, LSU (2005–2016):   114–34

14. Robert Neyland, Tennessee (1933–1934, 1936–1940, 1946–1952):   112–29–7

15. Tommy Tuberville, Ole Miss/Auburn (1995–2008):   110–60

16. Doug Dickey, Tennessee/Florida (1964–1978):   104–58–6

17. (tie) Pat Dye, Auburn (1981–1992):   99–39–4

18. (tie) Houston Nutt, Arkansas/Ole Miss (1998–2011):   99–74

19. Frank Thomas, Alabama (1933–1946):   98–21–7

20. Bernie Moore, LSU (1935–1947):   83–39–6

LEGEND
BEAR BRYANT

Paul William Bryant and the University of Alabama are inseparable. His 25-season transformation from respected coach to—in the words of former Crimson Tide coach Bill Curry—"divinity status" made it impossible to conjure an image of "the Bear" without his crimson sport coat.

But Bryant's skill is not best measured by what he accomplished at Alabama; it's what he did at the University of Kentucky that's truly unbelievable.

Consider: In 117 seasons *without* Bryant at the helm, the Wildcats have never won a conference title outright. They've never won 11 games in a season. They've never put together three consecutive seasons of eight wins or more. They've never finished in the Top 25 for more than two consecutive seasons. They've only won two bowl games vs. ranked opponents. You get it, right?

Well, in eight seasons under Bryant, the same program won an SEC title with an 11-victory season in 1950. The Wildcats also finished above .500 in each year, including three consecutive seasons of at least eight wins, 1949 to 1951. They were ranked at the end of the year five consecutive times, from 1949 to 1953. They beat No. 1 Oklahoma in the 1951 Sugar Bowl and No. 10 TCU in the 1952 Cotton Bowl.

Those Kentucky accolades alone would've been enough for a spot in the Hall of Fame. But when you throw in an undefeated season at Texas A&M and a quarter-century of destruction at Alabama, you've got what the kids call the "GOAT": Greatest of All Time.

Bryant began as No. 11—as in, the 11th of 12 kids in a poor family from Moro Bottom, Arkansas. As a teenager he earned his nickname by wrestling a carnival bear in a $1 contest.

In his own words to the *New York Times*: "The guy who was supposed to wrestle the bear didn't show up, so they egged me on. They let me and my friends into the picture show free, and I wrestled this scrawny bear to the floor. I went around later to get my money, but the guy with the bear had flown the coop. All I got out of the whole thing was a nickname."

As he grew older, his mother wished for him to be a preacher.

To that he said, "Coachin' and preachin' are a lot alike."

So, when he finished his standout playing career as a Crimson Tide end, he swiftly moved up the coaching ranks. Fewer than 10 years after his first gig as an Alabama assistant—including a World War II deployment—he was the head coach at the University of Maryland.

From there, life got awfully tough for the rest of the country's coaches. As the saying went, the Bear could take his team and beat yours, then take your team and beat his.

"Alabama's an itty-bitty state. And when he came, Alabama was down," former Bryant player and assistant coach Bill Oliver said in 2016. "If he had gone to Georgia and coached 25 years like he did at Alabama . . . I'd guarantee you he'd have won 12 national championships. I believe that. I really, really believe it. Vince Dooley was there, what, 25? Won one. And he had Herschel."

claim to fame was literally running through the Tennessee defense as an 18-year-old. Jackson did plenty of steamrolling, but his most memorable play required him to go over his opponents.

In 1982, Bear Bryant's final season at Alabama, the Crimson Tide had won nine consecutive games against the Auburn Tigers. Thanks to the superfrosh wearing uniform No. 34, the power balance was about to shift.

Facing a 22–17 deficit with 7:06 to play, Auburn got the ball at its own 33-yard line. The Tigers had been outgained by nearly 300 yards to that point.

Quarterback Randy Campbell proceeded to engineer a molasses-slow drive that included a third-and-14 conversion as well as an interception-turned-pass-interference-call that moved the ball to the Alabama 9-yard line.

A false start bumped the ball back, then Campbell threw incomplete to the end zone. Following an option pitch to Jackson that got the penalty yards back, Campbell threw underneath on third down to Jackson, who somersaulted over a pair of Tide tacklers and crash-landed just short of the end zone.

Upset by the referees' spot, Jackson slammed the football into the turf with both hands. He would only get one more chance to win it.

On fourth-and-goal from the 1-yard line, Campbell opened right and then spun to hand Jackson the ball. The freshman had a full head of steam, and he leapt over the line, his body horizontal in the air.

The Crimson Tide was able to slow his momentum enough that—for a split second—it looked like Jackson might be stopped shy of the end zone. But his 200-plus-pound frame created enough force to fall forward, and Auburn claimed a 23–22 win, its first over Alabama in 10 tries.

"He got in on that last wiggle," coach Pat Dye said while rewatching the play afterward.

1985 IRON BOWL ("THE KICK")

In the time it took for a football to travel 52 yards through the air, Bo Jackson's broken ribs were forgotten, and Van Tiffin became a household name in Alabama.

The 50th Iron Bowl was played before a national audience on ABC, and viewers witnessed an unforgettable fourth quarter. Jackson, playing with two fractured ribs, overcame a slow start to gallop for 142 yards and two scores. Those points provided a 17–16 lead for No. 7 Auburn, but unranked Alabama struck back with a 74-yard touchdown run by Gene Jelks.

Jackson keyed the Tigers' subsequent 70-yard response, and—after both teams had missed 2-point conversion attempts—the scoreboard read Auburn 23, Alabama 22 with 0:57 on the clock.

The circumstances were familiar to Crimson Tide quarterback Mike Shula, who would return to Tuscaloosa as head coach in 2003. The junior southpaw had engineered a five-play, 71-yard touchdown drive with 50 seconds left to beat Georgia earlier in the year.

But this one would not progress as smoothly, as the Tide still faced fourth-and-4 from deep in its own territory.

Then, the offensive play of the day came down from the coaches' booth: a reverse.

"There was silence on the phone," offensive coordinator George Henshaw said of the surprise call. "I thought it would work because they had been pursuing so hard from the backside all day."

Shula pitched to Jelks, who ran right and then handed the ball to wide receiver Albert Bell, who scampered the opposite direction. The trick play went for 20 yards, and then Shula completed another pass into Auburn territory with six seconds remaining.

On came Tiffin, who had no idea he was about to earn a lifetime of free drinks in Tuscaloosa County.

The goalposts stood 52 yards away. He'd missed wide left from the same distance earlier in the game, but there wasn't much time to think about it. Tiffin plunked his 1-inch tee on the ground, readjusted it, then took four sloppy steps away from the ball.

Before the radio announcers could properly set the scene, the ball was snapped. A diving Auburn defensive back had an early jump—probably too early, though a flag was not thrown—and dove for the ball. Tiffin made contact with a millisecond to spare.

The kick was a bomb: straight down the middle, and it probably would have cleared the crossbar from 60.

LEGEND

BO JACKSON

The greatest player in Auburn history grew up a huge Alabama Crimson Tide fan.

Who knows? Bo Jackson might have led the Tide to a national title in Bear Bryant's final season, but there was a one major snag: the Bear didn't like playing freshmen. And not even a scary-good athlete such as Jackson was going to see the field early.

Aside from his career as a two-way gridiron destroyer and a no-hitter-tossing pitcher, Jackson was a two-time Alabama state champion in the decathlon at McAdory High in small-town McCalla. There was likely some skepticism about his ability to be a star running back in the SEC, but there were no doubts about his superior athleticism.

As Bryant's health slipped, Pat Dye's staff pounced; longtime Alabama media personality—and current SEC Network star—Paul Finebaum recalled Auburn assistants mailing copies of unflattering Bryant photos ("He just looked terribly old") to every Tigers recruit.

In person, they had a simple pitch for Jackson: If you're the best running back we have, you'll play.

Whatever the primary reason, Jackson spurned his childhood team and drove to Lee County to begin his college football career. Unlike Georgia's Herschel Walker, who mostly failed to meet expectations during his first Georgia camp, Jackson was electrifying from the outset.

"I turned around to hand him the ball, and he was already gone past me," quarterback Randy Campbell recalled. "I told the coaches, 'He's lining up too close.'"

He wasn't. And he made a swift climb to the top of the depth chart.

"The thing is, he was so much better than everybody," Campbell said. "Nobody went back to their rooms saying, 'I can't believe they put that freshman ahead of me.' It was like if I was playing quarterback and all of a sudden John Elway transferred to Auburn. It was that obvious."

Jackson helped Auburn reclaim Yellowhammer bragging rights after a long period under the Crimson Tide's thumb. It seemed he saved some of his wildest moments for the Iron Bowl; Auburn fans still smile upon hearing the phrase "Bo Over the Top," just as their faces get cloudy at mention of "Wrong Way Bo" (a critical missed blocking assignment in '83) or "the Kick" (a game-winning Tide field goal that nullified Jackson's two touchdowns on cracked ribs in '84).

There was also a Sugar Bowl win over Michigan and the 1985 Heisman Trophy. But football wasn't Jackson's only love at Auburn. He also starred on the baseball diamond, where he batted .401 as a junior and collected 28 career home runs.

"Bo was without question the most incredible specimen I have ever seen in virtually every measurable physical category—speed, strength,

eye-hand coordination, leaping ability, arm strength," baseball coach Hal Baird said. "You name it, Bo was off the charts."

Following his time at Auburn, he was a two-sport professional star, becoming the first—and still only—athlete to be named both an MLB All-Star and an NFL Pro Bowler. His freak athletic ability resulted in too many iconic moments to cover here. Among them: a lightspeed 91-yard touchdown run on *Monday Night Football*, a baseball bat snapping in half across his knee, and a Spider-Man-esque outfield wall climb after sprinting to make a catch. All of it took on mythical status.

He became a pop-culture sensation. Nike ads insisted "BO KNOWS." *Tecmo Bowl* turned him into the Incredible Hulk, and he did his best real-life impression on Sundays.

Though his football career ended prematurely after a 1991 hip injury, his legend lives on across the world.

"I loved being better than the next guy," he said in 2017. "I enjoyed watching people's eyes jump out of their heads watching me do something that was normal to me."

Alabama players stormed the field and lifted Tiffin into the air as the broadcast team of Doug Layton and Paul Kennedy echoed each other: "It's good!" "It's GOOD!" "It's good!" "It's GOOD!" "It's good!" "It's GOOD!"

"Van Tiffin has kicked a 52-yard field goal," Kennedy finally mustered, "and the state of Alabama is crimson!"

1989 IRON BOWL

The fall of the Berlin Wall began November 9, 1989. The fall of the Birmingham Wall followed one month later.

That's how Auburn coach Pat Dye saw it, anyway: "It was like they had been freed and let out of bondage," he said postgame, "just having this game at Auburn."

Birmingham's Legion Field had served as the "neutral" site for the Iron Bowl between 1948 and 1988. But, as Auburn Board of Trustees member Morris Savage famously put it, the venue—which featured game-day workers wearing crimson and had a bust of Bear Bryant outside—was "as neutral as the beaches of Normandy were on D-Day."

It's now tradition for the Iron Bowl to swap between Tuscaloosa and Auburn on an annual basis, but the Tigers had to fight their way into that arrangement. Even when the Legion Field contract ran out in 1988, Alabama claimed there were four more years to go (Bryant had handwritten the amendment on Alabama's contract, but it did not appear on Auburn's).

As a compromise, Auburn agreed to meet at Legion one final time in 1991, but after that, the Tigers had the freedom to host their biennial game wherever they wanted.

Auburn sports information director David Housel gave a somewhat harrowing explanation of the process to the *Columbus Ledger-Inquirer* years later: "It's a good thing [young Auburn fans] don't understand [the importance] because that's what Dec. 2, 1989 was all about—so they wouldn't have to understand, be forced to go to Birmingham, be forced to play your biggest game of the year on your opponent's home field, be forced to go to a place where you weren't really wanted. . . . These kids don't know. Thank God they don't know."

In the immediate aftermath of the famous '89 game, *Los Angeles Times* writer Gene Wojciechowski dubbed Auburn "Hyperbole Central" and mocked Dye for a postgame thank-you speech that included just about every person under the sun.

"What he should have done," Wojciechowski wrote, "is thanked Alabama for saving its worst for last."

Entering the game, Alabama coach Bill Curry was finally living up to Bear Bryant's legacy. He'd struggled to earn respect from alumni through his first two seasons, but 1989 was setting up to be special. The Crimson Tide was 10–0 and ranked No. 2; it was the best 'Bama team of the decade, and Curry was in good position to end the school's three-game losing streak to Auburn.

Then, the Crimson Tide walked into a war zone.

Auburn's famed Tiger Walk was so intense that several players on the home side began hyperventilating. Inside the stadium, fans shook blue pom-poms so vigorously that a blue mist seemed to overtake the sky.

The details of Auburn's 30–20 win are rarely discussed (the No. 11-ranked Tigers ripped off 20 consecutive second-half points to pull the upset), as the off-field spectacle was sufficient enough for history books.

National media may have been skeptical of the sentiment from Dye and others, but those who witnessed the scene in person were blown away.

"Dramatic? Sure," wrote AL.com's Kevin Scarbinsky. "Over the top? Not if you were there."

2010 IRON BOWL ("THE CAMBACK")

Of all the notable offensive performances in Iron Bowl history, none compares to what Cam Newton accomplished after falling behind Alabama by 24 points.

Newton's No. 2-ranked Auburn squad was averaging more than 500 yards per game entering the Iron Bowl, and the Tigers were confident they could steamroll the defending national champions. Alabama had opened the year at No. 1, but losses to South Carolina and LSU had pushed the Tide out of the title picture.

As always, the facts on paper meant diddly-squat when the SEC's best rivalry game kicked off.

Auburn quarterback Cam Newton silences his doubters after a legendary "Cam-back" against Alabama in 2010. The game marked the biggest comeback in Auburn history and Alabama's first home loss in 21 games.
AP PHOTO/DAVE MARTIN

By the end of the first quarter, Auburn had minus-3 yards from scrimmage in three drives. The Tigers soon faced a 24–0 deficit, and trailed 24–7 at the half.

No team had buried Auburn like that. Alabama was a tad uneasy.

"We knew that we were going to have to score more than 24 to win it, just because Cam is so good of a player," quarterback Greg McElroy said. "At some point, he was going to make a few plays. It was inevitable."

McElroy, who had never lost at home, watched his fears come true. Newton quickly added to his 36-yard first-half touchdown toss, firing a 70-yarder to Terrell Zachary less than a minute into the second half. Later in the quarter, he punctuated a lengthy drive with a 1-yard dive into the end zone.

Suddenly, it was 24–21, and Alabama needed something—anything—to regain momentum after responding with a three-and-out drive.

Crimson prayers were swiftly answered. Auburn punt returner Quindarius Carr spun into a blindside hit by Alabama's Courtney Upshaw, who knocked the ball loose. 'Bama was back in prime scoring position, ball at the Tigers' 27.

Everyone will remember this game for Newton's heroics, but it would be an injustice to overlook the job Auburn's defense did during the comeback effort. Not only did the Tigers D hold Alabama to a field goal on the ensuing drive, it also stripped McElroy and star running back Mark Ingram on the 7-yard line and 19-yard line, respectively, in the first half to keep the game within reach.

When Newton and the Tigers offense took the field again, they would need just one more touchdown drive to seal an all-time great comeback.

It came with the help of a gamble. Facing fourth-and-3 from the Alabama 47 with 13:41 remaining, Newton fired a bullet to Darvin Adams for 9 yards. Five plays later, Newton hit Philip Lutzenkirchen for a 7-yard score, and Wes Bynum's extra point gave Auburn a 28–27 lead.

Alabama's offense threatened one final time, but Auburn's T'Sharvan Bell ended the scare with a third-down sack that knocked the Tide out of field goal position and knocked McElroy out of the game with a concussion.

Coach Gene Chizik and offensive coordinator Gus Malzahn took the biggest risk of the game minutes later. Auburn faced fourth-and-inches at its own 36-yard line with 3:08 to play. Instead of punting the ball away to 'Bama and backup quarterback AJ McCarron, the Tigers went for it, with Newton taking a shotgun snap and bursting past the first-down marker for 3 yards.

The result was the largest comeback in Auburn history and Alabama's first loss at Bryant-Denny Stadium in 21 games. Newton ran around the stadium with his hand over his mouth, silencing a crowd of nearly 102,000 that once saw a Crimson Tide upset as imminent.

"Cameron Newton is as physically and mentally tough as anyone I've been around," Chizik told reporters. "Period."

2013 IRON BOWL ("THE KICK SIX")

The clock read 0:00, and—for just a moment—the greatest play in SEC history was doomed to nonexistence.

LEGEND
CAM NEWTON

As Cam Newton took the field for warm-ups before the 2010 Iron Bowl, Bryant-Denny Stadium's speakers began blaring the Steve Miller Band hit "Take the Money and Run." In case the target wasn't obvious, Dusty Springfield's "Son of a Preacher Man" followed.

Newton didn't say whether he noticed, but others did; Alabama fired its mischievous stadium staffer days after Auburn's 28–27 win.

Auburn's 6-foot-6, 250-pound quarterback was indeed the son of a preacher man, Cecil Newton, whom the NCAA ruled had requested $180,000 from Mississippi State during his son's recruitment from Blinn (Texas) College.

The governing body cleared Newton (the player) and Auburn of any wrongdoing, but the junior was guilty of one crime: running all over SEC defenses that autumn. Never before had the conference seen such crazy individual statistics: 4,534 combined passing, rushing, and receiving yards, plus 51 total touchdowns. All while leading Auburn to a perfect 14–0 record and its first national title in more than a half-century.

It was an unbelievable year considering Newton's circumstances the previous season. A native of the Atlanta area, he signed with Florida in 2007 and was arrested one year later for possession of a stolen laptop. Facing expulsion, Newton transferred to Blinn—until then, a largely unknown entity—and spent his nights trying to sleep while cows mooed outside his window.

"I believe it was all calculated," Blinn communications director Jeff Tilley said. "If you want to pick somewhere that's secluded, to get away from the limelight, to take care of business, I can't think of a more perfect place."

Newton patched his reputation back together, got his associate's degree, and began listening to offers from Division I schools. It was at that point that his father, Cecil, apparently began soliciting cash for his son's signature.

The dual-threat quarterback eventually signed with Auburn—it was his father's decision, he said—and promptly destroyed the rest of the league. Heisman Trophy voting had rarely been so lopsided, but the story was not the margin; it was that Newton's father was forced to watch from home while the NCAA, the Mississippi Secretary of State's office, and the FBI continued their investigations.

"There was no doubt Newton would win the Heisman," Associated Press coverage read. "Whether he gets to keep it is still uncertain."

The official verdict never changed. Newton still has his Heisman. Auburn still has its national championship. But ask SEC fans outside Lee County for their opinion, and they'll come to a different conclusion.

Not that any of the controversy kept Newton from even greater success; he was selected No. 1 overall in the 2011 NFL Draft and became just the eighth man to win both the Heisman and NFL MVP.

"Thank you for supporting me in an unwavering way for so much of my career," Newton said after winning the latter award in January 2016. "I would also like to thank every person that has doubted me because you make me better."

Auburn fans flood the field at Jordan-Hare Stadium after a stunning "Kick Six" victory over Alabama in 2013. The game is considered by many to be the best in Iron Bowl history. AP PHOTO/SKIP MARTIN

Alabama running back T. J. Yeldon had stepped out of bounds at the Auburn 40-yard line as the final second slipped away, but the officiating crew gave the play a second look. 'Bama fans hoped for an extra tick. Auburn fans prayed for overtime.

The home crowd at Jordan-Hare Stadium let out a groan when head referee Matt Austin announced that one second would go back on the scoreboard.

Both senior Cade Foster (0-for-3 on the night) and freshman Adam Griffith warmed up to attempt the 57-yard field goal. Alabama coach Nick Saban decided on Griffith, a Polish immigrant who had attempted only two career field goals.

CBS analyst Gary Danielson began explaining how Auburn would attempt to defend a Hail Mary when he realized Alabama's plan.

"They're gonna try a field goal?" he yelped.

Auburn coach Gus Malzahn called for a safe defense that would combat a potential fake. Senior defensive back Ryan Smith jogged to the end zone in case Griffith came up short. Then, Malzahn changed his

Tigers defensive back Chris Davis runs back an errant Alabama field goal attempt 100 yards for a touchdown. "We're a team of destiny," Davis said afterward.
AP PHOTO/DAVE MARTIN

mind and called time-out. The Tigers swapped personnel, putting senior cornerback Chris Davis in the back of the end zone. Meanwhile, Alabama settled on eight offensive linemen in order to prevent their second blocked kick of the game.

The snap was good. The hold was good. Griffith drilled the ball. Everyone watched it sail toward glory.

It wasn't quite long enough. Davis caught the football roughly 9 yards deep in the end zone and began taking a path toward the right side of the field. Near the 10-yard line, he juked to his left as a pair of Alabama players flew by. He tiptoed the sideline and turned on the burners. Alabama's holder, Cody Mandell, was too late to put a hand on him.

Viewers across the country had hair standing on their skin as Davis reached the end zone and disappeared beneath a pile of teammates.

Toomer's Corner gets a toilet-paper makeover following Auburn's win over Alabama in 2013. "Rolling the corner" is one of the SEC's most well-known traditions.
AP PHOTO/BUTCH DILL

"I knew when I caught the ball I would have room to run," he said afterward. "I knew they would have big guys on the field to protect on the field goal. When I looked back, I said, 'I can't believe this.'"

Auburn, which had finished 3–9 the season before and had lost the past two Iron Bowls by a combined 77 points, was headed to Atlanta with at least a No. 3 ranking and a chance to reach the national title game.

Thousands of fans dressed in blue and orange swarmed the field, filling it nearly to the brim in a scene that would be endlessly replayed on ESPN in the following days. Alabama fans stood in stunned silence, mouths agape, as television cameras panned around the madness.

All of this two weeks after "the Immaculate Deflection," a tipped fourth-and-18 heave from quarterback Nick Marshall to receiver Ricardo Louis that beat Georgia in front of a similarly delirious group of more than 87,000 at Jordan-Hare.

Only a once-in-a-lifetime twist could top it.

"I thought the most risky part was a [blocked kick]," Danielson commented. "I guess there were two risky parts."

Davis's runback will outlast any other moment from the game—and rightfully so—but it would not have been possible without a touchdown pass moments earlier that technically shouldn't have counted.

With 39 seconds remaining and the Tigers facing a 28–21 deficit, quarterback Nick Marshall had the perfect call in mind.

The play was a read option with an *extra* option tacked on: If Marshall kept the ball instead of handing off, he could run . . . or he could pull up and throw to wideout Sammie Coates. The Alabama defense was unaware of that last bit.

"We ran the same play three times," Marshall said later. "The first time we ran it, I got like 6 yards. The second time, we got a first down. But as I carried out my fake [on the second attempt], I saw the corner come up and try to tackle me and let the receiver go. So I told coach."

Trailing by 7 with the SEC West title on the line, Marshall got the green light from Malzahn. He pulled the ball away from halfback Tre Mason and began sprinting left toward the line of scrimmage. Just as his front foot crossed the line, Marshall switched the ball from his left to his right hand and let loose an ugly duckling that landed in Coates's arms; no one was within 10 yards of the receiver, who waltzed into the end zone for the tying score.

"We had it open during the season, but I never threw it to him," Marshall said. "Coach always told me we were going to get one. It just happened to be that one against Alabama."

Upon review, the referees had missed the fact that at least one Auburn offensive lineman was more than 3 yards past the line of scrimmage at the time of the throw. It was, by the book, an infraction. But at the time, that call was an admitted blind spot for officiating crews around the country (the NCAA began emphasizing enforcement of the rule three years later).

Marshall and the Auburn spread offense went on to terrorize Missouri in the SEC championship game, racking up 677 total yards in a 59–42 thriller. The Tigers found plenty of success against Florida State in the national title contest, too. Mason scored a go-ahead 37-yard touchdown run with 1:19 remaining, but the Seminoles mounted a game-winning response that ended the SEC's streak of consecutive national titles at seven.

It was rare—and likely unprecedented in college football—that a 99-yard touchdown pass was not the longest play of the game, but AJ McCarron and Amari Cooper's dramatic fourth-quarter connection quickly faded from memory as Auburn's celebration began.

Fresh off a *Sports Illustrated* cover that wondered, "Is it time to think about AJ McCarron as one of the best ever?," the two-time national champion quarterback appeared to have thrown off the magazine's famous jinx with a true Heisman moment.

The game was tied, 21–21, with 10:42 remaining, and Auburn had just downed a punt at the Alabama 1-yard line. Instead of a conservative play call, 'Bama went for the jugular; McCarron playacted to his left, then heaved a rainbow down the right sideline. Cooper hauled it in between two Tigers before racing to the end zone.

It was the first 99-yard pass in Alabama history, and McCarron celebrated like it; he sprinted down the field, screaming and holding his fist high.

'Bama appeared headed for a third consecutive SEC championship game and a chance at its third consecutive national title. McCarron was a legitimate threat to sneak the Heisman away from Florida State's Jameis Winston. For those wearing crimson, the Iron Bowl was unfolding just as they'd imagined.

Postgame, the "what ifs" were brutal: four missed field goals, including one from 33 yards. A failed fourth-and-1 at the Auburn 13. A dropped touchdown by Cooper. And, for only the fourth time in NCAA history, a field goal returned 100 yards.

It all made perfect sense to Auburn.

"We're a team of destiny," Chris Davis said. "We won't take no for an answer."

PART 3: HAIL MARY AND OTHER PRAYERS

The Southern debut of Notre Dame's famed "Four Horsemen" coincided with the national debut of football's Hail Mary, and the city of Atlanta served as witness to both.

On October 28, 1922, the story goes, Notre Dame lineman Noble Kizer asked his Fighting Irish teammates to pray before a fourth-and-goal play vs. Georgia Tech. The Irish converted. Later, on a third-and-goal, Notre Dame prayed again. Another conversion.

"Say," Kizer said, per the account of teammate Jim Crowley, "that Hail Mary is the best play we've got."

Two years later, the Irish's core four of Crowley, Elmer Layden, Don Miller, and Harry Stuhldreher would receive their legendary "Four Horsemen" nickname from sportswriter Grantland Rice. Kizer's "Hail Mary" term would not stick, however. And it would not make a comeback until Dallas Cowboys quarterback Roger Staubach recoined it following a last-minute touchdown heave vs. the Minnesota Vikings in 1975.

Retroactively, there were a few SEC moments that deserved the prayerful moniker—perhaps most notably, an LSU touchdown pass that traveled 65 yards in the air to tie SMU in 1934—but the majority of the magic happened post-Staubach.

From Fran to Feleipe, here's a closer look at the SEC's answered prayers.

1959 AUBURN @ GEORGIA

If there's one play remaining in a game of backyard football, it's common for kids to huddle up and design the winning touchdown in the dirt.

In 1959, in the Deep South's Oldest Rivalry game, on fourth down, with the conference championship on the line and a sellout crowd screaming . . . Georgia Bulldogs quarterback Fran Tarkenton decided to channel his inner youth.

"I knew we had to show them something they had never seen before," Tarkenton said. "So I drew it right there in the huddle, running my finger over the grass."

Receivers Don Soberdash and Fred Brown were told to clog up the middle of the field. Meanwhile, tight end Bill Herron was told to hold his block for "four counts," jab right, then sprint to the left corner.

Tarkenton took the snap, stared down Soberdash and Brown, then whipped around to loft a pass to Herron. Auburn's backside defender had overcommitted to the middle, and the ball fell into Herron's paws for a 13-yard touchdown. Durward Pennington kicked the extra point and Georgia had a 14–13 win over an Auburn team that had claimed the national title in 1957 and gone unbeaten again in '58.

The Bulldogs, a measly 4–6 the previous season, were now perhaps the most shocking SEC champions in league history.

A key aspect of the turnaround was Georgia's slim figure. In '58, the Bulldogs were too fat to win. That changed in '59, per *Sports Illustrated*'s Kenneth Rudeen: "Abashed at the team's corpulence, Don Soberdash, the team captain, vowed there would be head knocking if anyone returned overweight in the fall; nobody did."

Of course, the talented Tarkenton was important, too. He and fellow quarterback Charlie Britt shredded defenses in Wally Butts's pass-first scheme. Tarkenton was particularly adept at avoiding rushers and throwing on the run. It's a skill he took to the NFL, where he retired with career records for pass attempts, completions, pass yards, touchdowns, rushing yards by a quarterback, and wins by a starting quarterback.

1965 ALABAMA @ GEORGIA

Pat Hodgson's knee hit the ground. Clear as day. In fact, both of his knees were down, and the official had a perfect angle to see it.

Georgia fans are quick to tell you that while Hodgson was on the turf, he hadn't controlled the ball long enough for the play to be ruled dead. Whatever the reason, play continued. His lateral to "Bullet" Bob Taylor led to a 73-yard touchdown, and the ensuing 2-point conversion gave Georgia an 18–17 upset of No. 5 Alabama.

It's true that Hodgson—who had run a curl route to snag Kirby Moore's pass near Georgia's 35-yard line—appeared to bobble the football as he went to the ground. But it's also clear he had enough "possession" to complete a perfect pitch to Taylor. Needless to say, Alabama coach Bear Bryant was not happy about the call when he saw the video replay.

His 33-year-old adversary, Georgia coach Vince Dooley, had drawn up the hook-and-ladder in his playbook four years earlier after watching Georgia Tech use it against Auburn.

"I thank them very much," Dooley said after the win. "We practiced it for two weeks, but I thought it would be 1980 before I'd have the nerve to call it in a game."

Alabama, the defending national champion, was heavily favored entering the game at Sanford Stadium. The Crimson Tide had whipped the Bulldogs, 31–3, the year prior, and figured to do so again in front of a national audience on NBC.

But the 'Dawgs defense helped stake Georgia to a 10–0 halftime lead, with the lone touchdown coming on a 55-yard interception return by lineman George Patton. Dooley, in his second year as head coach, appeared to have Bryant beat on opening weekend.

The Bear swung back in a hurry. Alabama produced three consecutive scores to take a 17–10 lead, and the Bulldogs were in bad shape. Quarterback Preston Ridlehuber had been pulled early alongside the rest of the first-team offense, and Moore—playing in his first varsity game—had not led a scoring drive since the first quarter.

With a little more than three minutes remaining and the ball at the Georgia 27-yard line, Dooley dialed up some trickery on the first play. Moore dropped back and fired to Hodgson, who fell forward onto his knees before flipping the ball to Taylor and creating the most famous (until January 2018, at least) moment in the Alabama-Georgia rivalry.

Instead of settling for a tie, Dooley kept his offense on the field, and Moore found Hodgson in the back of the end zone for the winning points.

Once the clock hit 0:00, students poured onto the field and players carried Dooley off it. It was the first major victory of his young career, and he used that win—plus a defeat of No. 7 Michigan two weeks later—to reestablish Georgia as a perennial contender.

1972 OLE MISS @ LSU

With four seconds left on the game clock and LSU facing a 16–10 deficit, Bert Jones dropped back to pass from the Ole Miss 10-yard line. Everyone in Tiger Stadium knew it was the home team's last gasp. Jones's bullet pass shot toward intended receiver Jimmy LeDoux and then fell to the turf, incomplete.

Ole Miss defensive back Mickey Fratesi jumped up and down in celebration. Jones was beside himself; he yelled at the referees for a pass interference call, but got none. Louisiana State's undefeated season was no more. Or was it?

The quarterback looked up at the stadium game clock, which still—somehow—had one second on it. Jones, the "Ruston Rifle," would get one more chance to complete a game-winning 80-yard drive and propel LSU to a 7–0 record and its 12th consecutive win.

On the sideline during a time-out, LSU coach Charlie McClendon called for a play the Tigers had been using as a 2-point conversion attempt in practice. Coaches and teammates later said their quarterback exuded confidence, but he didn't recall it that way.

"Coach Mac said I winked at him on the sidelines," Jones said. "I really think it was probably a nervous twitch."

On the ensuing play, Jones looked to his left, hesitated, then launched the football to halfback Brad Davis, who was sprinting toward the sideline. Davis lost the ball in the stadium lights and "just threw [his] hands up" to haul in the throw. He crashed over the pylon as an Ole Miss defender dragged him down. The side judge raised his hands to signal a touchdown, and Tiger Stadium exploded with noise.

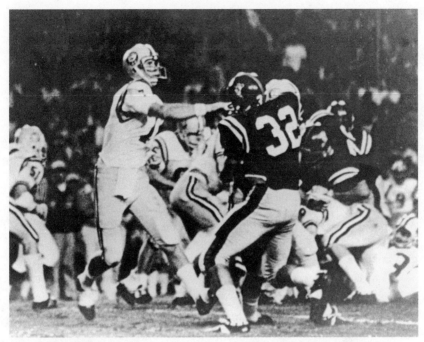

LSU quarterback Bert Jones passes against Ole Miss. He and the Tigers made the most of some controversial timekeeping to beat the Rebels 17–16 in Baton Rouge. LSU ATHLETICS

The chaos—several fans and players milled around the field for minutes—was understandable, but the scoreboard still read LSU 16, Ole Miss 16. The Tigers needed an extra point to win. Rusty Jackson toed it home and the Tigers had an improbable victory.

"They'll never believe this one in the far reaches of the Southeastern Conference," *Shreveport Times* editor Bill McIntyre wrote. "I'm here even now, and I don't believe it. Not at all."

He added: "LSU 17, Ole Miss 16. A game won not in the final minute, nor in the final second. But after the ball game was over. Minus Zero Hour."

Unsurprisingly, the ending was controversial for Rebels fans. The official recap in Ole Miss's season summary read "Ole Miss 16, LSU 10+7," and provided a healthy dose of skepticism: "Was it an itchy finger triggering the clock guarding the game in Tiger Stadium last November 4 that was at fault, or did unbeaten LSU actually have a second to play?"

The state of Mississippi summed it up best when it put a highway sign on its border: "You are now entering Louisiana. Set your clocks back four seconds."

Jones found plenty of humor in the situation.

"People think that it was either my father or my brother running the clock," he said a few years later. "Really, it wasn't anything like that. It was a distant cousin of mine."

1980 GEORGIA VS. FLORIDA ("RUN, LINDSAY!")

The World's Largest Outdoor Cocktail Party was in full swing, but Georgia's championship-caliber offense was not.

Florida, a big underdog, had scored 11 unanswered points to take a 21–20 lead over the Bulldogs. Star freshman running back Herschel Walker was essentially a nonfactor as Georgia found itself deep in its own territory with 1:03 remaining and little hope for victory.

On third down from his own 8-yard line, quarterback Buck Belue faked a handoff—a pointless wrinkle, given the situation—and was quickly flushed out of the pocket to his right. He kept his eyes downfield and saw a white jersey streaking toward the middle.

It was Lindsay Scott, a junior receiver who had yet to score a touchdown on the season.

Belue pointed at Scott, a move that meant Scott was supposed to "sit" where he was instead of continuing his path. The two players had never discussed the gesture, per Belue. But Scott got the gist, and he halted to collect a bullet from his quarterback.

"He made the catch, and I thought, 'First down!'" Belue said. "We're in business!"

Scott had much more in mind. His feet hit the ground with his body facing the line of scrimmage. He spun to his right, nearly stumbled, and began sprinting toward the open field. There were plenty of Gators in the vicinity, but Scott blew them away.

Up in the radio booth, Georgia play-by-play man Larry Munson began counting the yard markers ("The 50! 45! 40!") until adrenaline overtook him.

"RUN, LINDSAY!" he yelled.

When Scott reached the end zone, he was swarmed by at least a dozen bystanders. His teammates—almost the entire roster, judging by the mass of white uniforms—had sprinted down the sideline and began mobbing him, too. Belue testified that he felt the Gator Bowl turf shaking as he made his way to join the celebration.

The touchdown gave Georgia a 26–21 win and propelled the Bulldogs from No. 2 to No. 1 in the following week's Top 25 polls. The 'Dawgs would win their final two regular-season games before claiming the national championship with a 17–10 Sugar Bowl win over Notre Dame.

Munson had plenty of famous radio calls, but none was as dangerous as Scott's 92-yard touchdown reception.

"I broke my chair," he said later. "I came right through a chair. A metal steel chair with about a 5-inch cushion. I broke it. The booth came apart. The stadium, well, the stadium fell down. Now they do have to renovate this thing. They'll have to rebuild it now."

1983 EGG BOWL ("THE IMMACULATE DEFLECTION")

"The Hand of God" was a tongue-in-cheek name for Diego Maradona's infamous handball goal in the 1986 World Cup. Three years earlier, the phrase could've been unironically used to describe the final play of the Egg Bowl.

Needing a field goal to beat in-state rival Ole Miss, Mississippi State lined one up from 27 yards away. On most Saturdays this would be a cinch. Problem was, Jackson's Veterans Memorial Stadium was ground zero for a Mississippi tempest. Winds had reached at least 40 miles per hour as MSU committed three consecutive turnovers to cough up a 16-point lead.

Another unfortunate factor: the kick would take place in the south end of the horseshoe stadium, meaning there were no stands to keep out the elements.

Still . . . 27 yards. Even in 1983, that was a chip shot. And freshman kicker Artie Cosby had already connected on three field goals, including one from 51 yards (though that one was on the north end).

When the time came for attempt No. 4, Cosby did his job to perfection. His kick was powerful and sky-high, easily good from 50 or farther on a normal day. The football was headed straight between the goalposts when that pesky "Hand of God" reached out and swatted it away. Watching in real time, the ball appeared to be halted by a tractor beam before pinwheeling back toward the line of scrimmage. Locals deemed it "the Immaculate Deflection."

Cosby went on to become one of the best kickers in Bulldogs history, but the windblown kick will always be part of his legacy. He even owns a photo of the play, featuring his Bulldogs holder raising his arms as if to say, "It's good! . . . Right?"

In 2013—30 years afterward—he discussed the play with the Mississippi Sports Hall of Fame, and expressed regret that he didn't get a chance to kick the *other* direction at the end of the first half, when MSU was stopped near midfield.

"I had 70-yard range going that way. I had already kicked a kickoff into the stands," Cosby said. "I could have made that kick. I should have told Coach [Emory] Bellard, but I was a redshirt freshman and just didn't have the gumption to go up and tell him. I wish I had.

"I would much rather be remembered for that kick than the other one."

1991 TENNESSEE @ NOTRE DAME ("THE MIRACLE AT SOUTH BEND")

A football game can come down to a single yard. And, sometimes, it can come down to a single butt cheek.

Tennessee rallied from a 31–7 deficit at No. 5-ranked Notre Dame to claim a 35–34 lead in the contest's closing minutes. But the Fighting Irish had the ball, and they also had time: 3 minutes, 57 seconds, to be exact.

Quarterback Rick Mirer led an 11-play drive that put the Irish at the Tennessee 9-yard line with roughly half a minute to go. Facing fourth-and-3, coach Lou Holtz decided to run the clock down and attempt a game-winning field goal. One big problem, though: All-America specialist Craig Hentrich had injured his knee in the first half. Notre Dame would be relying on Rob Leonard, a walk-on from Decatur, Georgia, who had attempted only one extra point in his college career. The sophomore wasn't even listed in Notre Dame's media guide.

Holtz put both hands around Leonard's helmet, drew him in close, and delivered some words of inspiration.

"It was a wonderful feeling going out there and having that opportunity, knowing the game rested on me," Leonard said afterward.

On the Tennessee side, Jeremy Lincoln prepared himself for a block attempt. Lined up on the far right of the formation, he got a great jump—too great. Lincoln, a track star, overran the holder. The kick went up ("The second I kicked it, I thought it was good," Leonard said) and ricocheted off Lincoln's rump.

The affected football still had the distance but wobbled wide right of the goalpost. Lincoln's oversized derriere had preserved the 35–34 win.

"I thank my mom for giving me a big butt," Lincoln told reporters. "When I go home she says, 'You've got a big butt.' I tell her, 'I can't help it. You gave it to me.' I put it to good use this time."

No visiting team had ever rallied from 24 down to beat the Fighting Irish at Notre Dame Stadium. It's still referred to as "the Miracle at South Bend," and—unbeknownst to anyone at the time—it was Volunteers coach Johnny Majors's last major victory at Tennessee before health problems and the rise of Phillip Fulmer forced him out.

"The University of Tennessee has not had a more important, or bigger, comeback in our school's history," Majors proclaimed afterward.

2000 FLORIDA @ TENNESSEE

Steve Spurrier's final visit to Neyland Stadium as Florida coach resulted in a fittingly horrifying ending for the Knoxville faithful.

Entering the game, the Head Ball Coach had taken six of seven against the Volunteers. His Gators were perhaps the only team in the country that didn't need to worry much about the Vols' 23-game home winning streak (Florida had, after all, been the last team to prevail before the streak began).

So, with 2:14 left on the clock and 91 yards to go for the winning touchdown, UF was once again poised to play the heartbreaker. Quarterback Jesse Palmer took advantage of a conservative Vols defense, moving the Gators downfield at lightspeed before tossing what appeared to be the game-winning touchdown pass to Reche Caldwell.

It was not; Florida had an ineligible lineman downfield, and was forced to regroup with 28 seconds remaining. Spurrier decided to try a play the Gators had just put in that week: Wideout Jabar Gaffney would run to the goal line, turn around, and box out his defender like a basketball player. Palmer would deliver a quick strike to catch the defense off guard.

On second-and-goal from the 3-yard line, everything went to plan, except for one minor detail: Gaffney dropped the ball. It hit him in the chest and he held it for a moment, but Tennessee cornerback Willie Miles immediately knocked it to the ground.

After the game, Gaffney was confident he caught it. Miles said no way.

Line judge Al Matthews's opinion was the one that mattered most, and he didn't hesitate. His arms shot up to signal a touchdown at the same moment the ball fell to the ground. Any impartial person with a close look would have overturned the call, but college football was still five years away from instituting instant-replay review. The play stood, and Florida had a 27–23 win that would propel it to another SEC title.

"No question, God was smiling on us because the other team outplayed us," Spurrier told reporters. "And somehow we got more points."

Somehow, eh?

"Oh boy," CBS broadcaster Verne Lundquist said moments after the winning play, "is that going to be controversial."

2002 LSU @ KENTUCKY ("THE BLUEGRASS MIRACLE")

How "over" was Kentucky's game vs. LSU on November 9, 2002? Look no further than the bucket of ice water that Wildcats quarterback Jared Lorenzen and offensive tackle Antonio Hall dumped on coach Guy Morriss with two seconds remaining.

Kentucky held a 30–27 lead over the visitors, and seemingly every blue-clad being in Commonwealth Stadium assumed victory. Wildcats

LSU wide receiver Devery Henderson (9) celebrates after catching the game-winning Hail Mary pass against Kentucky. Scores of Wildcats fans were already running around the field, thinking their team had won.
STEVE FRANZ/LSU

fans were already pouring onto the field; they lined the end zones and sidelines in anticipation of a big win.

Louisiana State was stuck at its own 26-yard line. Coach Nick Saban had no choice but to call Dash Right 93 Berlin, which had never worked in practice.

The play called for quarterback Marcus Randall to roll right while receivers Michael Clayton, Reggie Robinson, and Devery Henderson sprinted down the field. The first two were supposed to tip the deep ball into the air while Henderson sprinted behind the mass of bodies to make the catch.

Turns out, it was Kentucky that provided the tip.

Randall dropped back, rolled to his right, and uncorked a pass that traveled roughly 55 yards in the air before it smacked a Wildcats paw and caromed toward Henderson. The junior bobbled it as he streaked between a pair of Kentucky defensive backs, then gathered the football and raised both arms high as he stormed into the end zone.

The matrix crashed; Jefferson Pilot Sports's broadcast flashed an incorrect graphic ("Kentucky 30, LSU 27—FINAL"). Pockets of Kentucky fans had run onto the field of play and were too stunned to retreat. Some Tigers piled on top of Henderson. Others taunted the Wildcats' supporters, who were tearing down one of the goalposts in mistaken celebration.

Louisiana State defensive coordinator Will Muschamp hadn't even been paying attention on the final play.

"I got to the bottom of the numbers, and I realized all these players are running by me," Muschamp he said later. "And I'm thinking, 'What in the world could our players be happy about right now?' And I realized Devery had made the catch. I was like a lot of Kentucky fans. They didn't realize we had scored either."

On a zoomed-in replay of Randall, cameras caught a wave of blue students rushing the field in celebration as the football was tipped. None of them paid any attention to the ball's fate until Randall raised his arms to signal a touchdown, at which point one screaming fan in a black suit abruptly halted and stared at the other end of the field, his smile gone. Another oblivious young man in a blue sweatshirt followed Randall down the field, his arms still triumphantly raised.

As Saban walked off the field, he appeared just as stunned as everyone else.

"I don't know what to say," he began. "I feel bad for Kentucky players, but, hey, this is a big moment for us, and I'm happy as heck for our team . . . Sometimes you've gotta be a little lucky, and I think that was our luck right there."

"The Bluegrass Miracle" won Henderson an ESPY award for "Best Play" the following summer.

"People don't really let you forget it," Henderson said on the 10th anniversary, near the conclusion of a nine-year NFL career. "Every time I go back to LSU, I get reminded of it even more. It was just great to be a part of something like that and just be remembered in history."

2002 GEORGIA @ AUBURN

Ten SEC championship games came and went without participation from the Georgia Bulldogs, including eight games played just outside Athens at Atlanta's Georgia Dome.

Such were the stakes for No. 7 Georgia as its potential game-winning drive at No. 24 Auburn came to a halt. Quarterback David Greene had guided the 'Dawgs into the opposing red zone, but a trio of incomplete passes and a false-start penalty resulted in fourth-and-15 at the Tigers' 19-yard line.

Down 21–17 with a minute and a half remaining, the Bulldogs had no use for a field goal; Greene would need to throw it.

"It sounds kind of weird, but the guys were calm and even laughing a little bit," he said postgame. "We were saying, 'This is it. The whole season is in our hands. We wouldn't want it any other way.'"

The All-SEC southpaw took a shotgun snap, briefly looked to his right, then lobbed the football toward the left corner of the end zone. At first glance the pass was too short; receiver Michael Johnson was forced to slow down as Auburn defender—and former Georgia signee—Horace Willis boxed him out.

But as the ball made its descent, the Jordan-Hare Stadium sod intervened. Willis stumbled. Johnson capitalized; the junior leapt high over his defender and cradled the football for his second career touchdown catch.

Georgia, which had watched rivals Florida and Tennessee take the first 10 SEC East titles, claimed the divisional championship for the first time in history.

"We're going to Atlanta," linebacker Tony Gilbert said. "We should have been there a long, long time ago."

The Bulldogs demolished Arkansas in Atlanta, then defeated Florida State in the Sugar Bowl for a 13–1 record and a No. 3 ranking in the final polls. Second-year coach Mark Richt would eventually tally 145 career wins with the 'Dawgs, including another SEC championship in 2005.

2002 LSU @ ARKANSAS ("THE MIRACLE ON MARKHAM")

The winner of this Thanksgiving-week contest would earn the right to play Georgia in the 2002 SEC championship game, and—until the final half minute—it appeared as if LSU would ride its "Bluegrass Miracle" all the way to Atlanta.

Nick Saban's Tigers had held the Razorbacks' passing offense to 46 yards en route to building a 20–14 fourth-quarter lead. With 34 seconds remaining, the Hogs somehow had to travel nearly twice that length to win.

On came quarterback Matt Jones, who had completed just 2 of 14 passes with an interception in one of the worst performances of his career.

Jones took a shotgun snap from the Arkansas 19-yard line and strolled to his right, buying time by design. After surveying the field, he launched a deep ball that barely cleared an LSU defensive back's shoulder and fell into the arms of Richard Smith, who slid as he caught it at the LSU 31.

"Our play wasn't designed to go to Richard, but they let him get behind them," Jones told reporters afterward. "If I could have thrown the ball about 10 yards further we would have scored on that play."

With no time-outs to burn, Jones and the rest of the offense sprinted to the line of scrimmage and spiked the ball. On second-and-10, he fired a bullet to the right corner of the end zone, where DeCori Birmingham somehow hauled it in against airtight coverage for the winning touchdown.

Well, it was *supposed* to be the winning touchdown. The Razorbacks were flagged for excessive celebration, effectively turning the tie-breaking extra point into a 35-yard field goal.

David Carlton got plenty of leg behind the ball, which hooked left as it sailed over the goalpost. As fans held their breath, the officials quickly made their call: good.

Arkansas had a 21–20 lead with nine seconds to go. As everyone learned after the "Bluegrass Miracle," no lead was safe against LSU on the final play, but the Razorbacks stripped the ball from Marcus Randall in the end zone to punctuate their second SEC West title.

2007 AUBURN @ LSU

Louisiana State coach Les Miles was the spokesperson for Raising Cane's Chicken, and his commercials were well-known across the Pelican State. But his on-screen taste for another delicacy—grass—made him famous

LSU wide receiver Demetrius Byrd hauls in the game-winning touchdown throw from Matt Flynn. Byrd's catch bailed out coach Les Miles, who had lost track of time in the final minute. AP PHOTO/ALEX BRANDON

across the country. Perhaps it was the green stuff at Tiger Stadium that forced Miles's mind to malfunction against Auburn in 2007.

The teams had traded leads twice in the fourth quarter before LSU began the final drive, and Matt Flynn moved his offense down the field in short bursts. On second-and-8 from the Auburn 23, he hit Richard Dickson for a 1-yard gain with 45 seconds remaining.

Normally, that'd be plenty of time to regroup and get a few more plays off before attempting a game-winning field goal. That would also be too easy for Miles, dubbed LSU's "Mad Hatter" for his often-risky decisions. The Tigers inexplicably allowed the clock to run down to nine seconds before Flynn took his next snap. And instead of playing it conservative and preserving a potential 39-yard field goal, Flynn hucked the ball to the end zone.

Tigers wideout Demetrius Byrd was ready. Before the play he had been waving to the press box to get offensive coordinator Gary Crowton's attention. Byrd faced one-on-one coverage with plenty of room to get by Auburn's Jarraud Powers, and the sophomore created the fraction of separation he needed to haul in the winning touchdown as the clock ticked down to one second.

Baton Rouge erupted, but there was an obvious question for Miles, who still had one time-out in his pocket: What if the clock had run out on the final play?

"I did not expect it to come down to one second," he admitted. "I didn't have it timed out that far. Certainly it worked right."

A couple weeks after going 5-for-5 on fourth-down calls against Florida, the Flynn-to-Byrd high-wire act cemented Miles's reputation as a crazy man.

After all, this wasn't some meaningless late-season SEC contest; No. 4-ranked LSU had won 17 consecutive homes games coming into the matchup, and needed a victory to stay alive in the Bowl Championship Series race.

Flynn's flick did just that, and the Tigers went on to secure their third national title.

2010 TENNESSEE @ LSU

If you read the section just before this one—about LSU's last-second win over Auburn in 2007—you know that clock management was never Les Miles's forte. And yet, somehow, his mistakes tended to work in the Tigers' favor.

The scene: Miles's team trailed unranked Tennessee—a two-touchdown underdog—by the score of 14–10 in the final minute. On second-and-goal, quarterback Jordan Jefferson ran around the right side and was tackled near the 1-yard line. There were still 29 seconds on the clock, which was now running.

And running.

And running.

Minutes after celebrating a "win" with his teammates, Tennessee defensive lineman Chris Walker lies on the field, dejected, after a loss to LSU in 2010. An illegal participation penalty reversed both teams' fates with no time on the clock. AP PHOTO/PATRICK SEMANSKY

Both teams substituted players as the frustrated home crowd began roaring. The Tigers still had two downs to score the winning touchdown, but time for only one play.

With three seconds remaining, center T-Bob Hebert snapped the ball through the hands of Jefferson, who seemed distracted by something at the line of scrimmage. The football shot backward about 15 yards before a Tennessee player fell on it. Before the play was even dead, Vols players were rushing off the sideline to mob their teammates.

"It is over in Baton Rouge!" screamed CBS announcer Craig Bolerjack as Tennessee coach Derek Dooley hopped into the arms of his players and the band played a lively version of "Rocky Top."

More than a minute after the final play, head referee Marc Curles went to the sideline replay monitor. Whatever he saw, he saw quickly. He rushed onto the field to deliver the message.

"Illegal participation, on the defense," Curles said. "Twelve [men] on the field. Half the distance to the goal. Repeat third down."

The broadcast team went to a replay and counted the Tennessee players at the snap. There had not been 12. There had been 13.

A new energy overtook Tiger Stadium. Fans looked on with a combination of disbelief and bliss. Many had already headed toward the exits and were now standing in the aisles, dumbstruck.

To Miles's credit, he sprang into action, gathering his team to prepare for the second chance of a lifetime. He had already thrown his headset down—cutting off communication with offensive coordinator Gray Crowton—so he was forced to call the critical play by himself.

Dooley cussed on the Tennessee sideline as he strapped his headset back on. Both sides jogged out to the field, and LSU hurried to the line for a quick snap.

Jefferson spun and pitched left to running back Stevan Ridley, who powered over the goal line for the go-ahead score.

Now it was LSU's turn to go crazy. Players piled up in the end zone as Tennessee defenders fell to the ground in anguish. At least one Vols player wept openly. Dooley, who afterward said, "I have never hurt like this before," stormed onto the field for a quick handshake and then stormed off.

"A miracle!" Bolerjack shouted. "A miracle in Baton Rouge!"

2013 GEORGIA @ AUBURN ("THE PRAYER AT JORDAN-HARE")

A primary reason Auburn and Alabama's 2013 "Kick Six" game was so classic was the height of the stakes. Both teams were ranked among the top four in the country, and the winner advanced to the SEC title game.

Such a stage would not have been possible without a mind-bending 73-yard touchdown pass two weeks earlier.

Auburn's success was a big surprise in 2013. First-year coach Gus Malzahn had inherited a three-win team and swiftly developed a dangerous spread attack that highlighted dual-threat quarterback Nick Marshall and lightning-quick tailback Tre Mason. The Tigers' offensive line was

Auburn wide receiver Ricardo Louis grabs a 4th-and-18 throw from Nick Marshall and races into the end zone against Georgia in 2013. The improbable play became known as "The Prayer at Jordan-Hare."
AP PHOTO/*OPELIKA-AUBURN NEWS*, ALBERT CESARE

elite, and the defense was full of NFL prospects. It had been a season to remember for the No. 7-ranked team in the country.

A blown 20-point fourth-quarter lead and a 38–37 deficit against rival Georgia soured the mood. Auburn faced fourth-and-18 from its own 27 with little more than a half minute left. Fans eyed the exits.

As the crowd began its five stages of grief, Marshall took a shotgun snap, moseyed around for a few seconds, and tossed a deep ball to a group of three Georgia defenders. It was, by any hindsight-excluding grading system, a failure of a decision—especially with at least one nontargeted Tiger running wide open near midfield.

But the deed was done. The ball was out. And Auburn's national title hopes rode on receiver Ricardo Louis, who was in great position to watch the Bulldogs intercept the pass.

That's just what defensive back Tray Matthews was about to do when teammate Josh Harvey-Clemons reached up and tipped the football over Matthews's head. Louis, the Auburn receiver, raced past the pair and turned his head in time to grab the ball out of the air. He sprinted into the end zone as Jordan-Hare Stadium snapped from dead to delirious.

"I couldn't believe it," Louis said afterward. "It just landed right into my hands. I saw it once it got over my shoulder. It got tipped, I lost track of it . . . but when I looked over my shoulders, it was right there."

CBS announcer Gary Danielson christened it "a miracle of miracles." Georgia quarterback Aaron Murray—who, minutes earlier, had completed an all-time great comeback with a gutsy fourth-and-goal run—slammed his baseball cap into the turf.

After the final gun, fans rushed the field to celebrate "the Prayer at Jordan-Hare." Two weeks later in the Iron Bowl, they would do it again.

2015 ARKANSAS @ OLE MISS

This game might have been included among the SEC's greatest *without* its unbelievable fourth-down lateral. Arkansas and Ole Miss were tied at the end of the first (7–7), second (17–17), third (31–31), and fourth quarters (45–45). The final play in regulation was an attempted Razorbacks field goal that Rebels wide receiver Laquon Treadwell blocked with a perfectly timed leap.

If Mississippi could pull out a win in overtime, it would be one step closer to its first SEC West title and its first conference championship in 52 years.

Fans at Vaught-Hemingway Stadium were envisioning those milestones as Rebels quarterback Chad Kelly dashed across the goal line for a touchdown to open the extra period. The PAT made it 52–45, Ole Miss.

Kelly's counterpart, Arkansas quarterback Brandon Allen, had played the game of his life, throwing for more than 400 yards and five touchdowns as he took the field for the Hogs' rebuttal.

He threw incomplete on first down. Arkansas got called for delay of game before second down, and then Allen was sacked for a loss of 10 yards. His third-down pass fell to the turf.

Arkansas's chances of winning had cratered to zilch. The Hogs faced fourth-and-25 from the Rebels' 40-yard line.

Razorbacks coach Bret Bielema later thanked "divine intervention" for what happened next.

Allen took a shotgun snap and danced back to midfield. He faded to his left, then threw across the field to tight end Hunter Henry at the 25-yard line. The play appeared snuffed as Henry took a wallop, but he managed to toss a high-arcing lateral more than 15 yards behind him. The ball bounced off a lineman, slipped past a trio of Rebels defenders, and leapt into the mitts of Arkansas running back Alex Collins.

"I think the game is over," Collins said afterward. "Next thing I know, I see the ball flying through the sky."

Collins had a convoy of blockers in front of him, and he was able to weave his way past the first-down marker. As he was taken to the turf near the Ole Miss 9-yard line, he mistakenly thought the Hogs needed more yards, so he attempted to lateral the ball to tight end Dominique Reed. Thankfully for the Razorbacks, Reed fell on the ball at the 11.

Two plays later, Allen tossed his sixth touchdown pass of the game, finding a crossing Drew Morgan in the right side of the end zone. Bielema immediately decided to go for the win with a 2-point conversion attempt.

It was no good. Allen took a sack, and Vaught-Hemingway exploded.

Then, new life; Ole Miss linebacker Marquis Haynes had grabbed Allen's facemask during the takedown, giving the Hogs another shot just outside the Rebels' 1-yard line. Allen took advantage, keeping the ball himself and diving over a Mississippi defender for the winning points.

Arkansas's 53–52 win had a massive ripple effect on the season; it provided Alabama—which had lost to Ole Miss in September—a spot in the SEC championship game, and the Crimson Tide went on to win the national championship.

2016 TENNESSEE @ GEORGIA ("THE DOBBS-NAIL BOOT")

The Volunteers were already living a charmed life when they walked into Sanford Stadium. A fortuitous bounce of the football helped them survive an Appalachian State upset bid. A bundle of Virginia Tech turnovers helped turn a 14–0 deficit into victory at Bristol Motor Speedway. They successfully came back against Ohio and Florida in consecutive weeks at Neyland Stadium.

Amidst a crowd of other players, Tennessee wide receiver Jauan Jennings (15) reaches up to make a Hail Mary catch against Florida in 2016. "It's one of those moments in time that you'll remember forever," coach Butch Jones said.

Tennessee now faced still its biggest challenge yet: a 31–28 deficit with one play to run from Georgia's 43-yard line.

Coach Butch Jones thought about a short-throw-and-lateral play but changed his mind, saying afterward, "I had a feeling."

In came the call—"Big Ben"—and senior quarterback Josh Dobbs locked into his assignment: put the ball over the stem of the No. 2 receiver 5 yards deep in the end zone. So, the aerospace engineering major followed instructions and launched a rainbow to the perfect spot on the field. As the ball fell back to Earth, Dobbs tracked its flight and saw a pair of hands stretch out to grab it.

Those mitts belonged to Vols receiver Jauan Jennings, and he crashed to the end-zone turf between roughly six Georgia defenders for an improbable victory. Teammates mobbed him. Coach Jones, headset still on, ran toward Jennings before emotion overtook him and he crashed to his knees.

"It's one of those moments in time that you'll remember forever," Jones said. "From my vantage point, I could see him come down with the ball, landed on his back. All I could see was a mad rush to the field."

During the wild celebration, Jennings was lifted up on teammates' shoulders, and the wideout chucked the game-winning football back to the sideline. Dobbs tore himself away from the rest of the Vols to chase after the most valuable football of his career.

"It was a crazy play, stuff you dream about," Dobbs said in the locker room. "It was absolutely amazing."

2017 TENNESSEE @ FLORIDA

Florida was playing for overtime. Freshman quarterback Feleipe Franks had just thrown an interception that allowed Tennessee to tie the game 20–20, and Gators coach Jim McElwain was apparently content with running out the clock.

With two time-outs in his pocket, McElwain allowed 50 seconds to dwindle down to 9. The Swamp booed lustily.

Franks and the offense were marooned back at their own 34-yard line. Might they try to pick up 20 yards and give cannon-legged kicker Eddie Pineiro a shot to win it? Tennessee lined up its defensive backs deep, just in case.

Florida wide receiver Tyrie Cleveland turns Gators fans' boos into cheers with a game-winning touchdown catch vs. Tennessee in 2017. The throw from Feleipe Franks to Cleveland hung in the air for three and a half seconds.
GARY MCCULLOUGH/CSM CAL SPORT MEDIA VIA AP IMAGES

At the snap Franks worked upfield and glided to the right. The seconds ticked away. He neared the line of scrimmage, glanced to his left at a wide-open receiver near midfield, then appeared to think, "Screw it."

Flat-footed, he launched an unbelievable pass that sailed nearly 70 yards in the air.

"He's gonna go deep," said play-by-play man Brad Nessler, growing more excited as the camera followed the football's path. "And I mean deep!"

The bomb hung in the air for three and a half seconds, allowing wide receiver Tyrie Cleveland to slip past the back line of defense and make the game-winning catch in the end zone.

As the party of the year broke out around him, McElwain looked ready to call it a night. The beleaguered leader—who would be fired in

October—could barely muster a smile as CBS reporter Allie LaForce peppered him with questions.

Her final inquiry gave McElwain an opportunity to butter up Franks after his 63-yard touchdown.

"What did that freshman show you? Maybe that he was a little more like a veteran today?" LaForce asked.

McElwain very nearly rolled his eyes at the thought.

"No," he said, chuckling. "He showed me he can throw it a long ways."

PART 4:
THE CLASSICS

In other sections of this book, you can read about iconic moments, Iron Bowls, Hail Marys, and championships. But without the classics, the SEC story would be incomplete. These are the games that were so memorable, they stand on their own—separate from a common theme—and live on in the memories of fan bases across the South.

1929 YALE @ GEORGIA

Featuring a roster of small-town in-state players that included young men nicknamed "Jack the Ripper" and "Catfish," the Georgia Bulldogs were one of the Southern Conference's last great teams before the SEC was established in late 1932.

Georgia had a great northern challenge in 1929: stopping a 144-pound Yale running back with two nicknames. Albie Booth was known as "Little Boy Blue" and the "Mighty Atom," and his evasive style was well-known across the Ivy League. In a game against Army later in the season, he would run for 233 yards and be responsible for all of the Ivy Leaguers' points in a come-from-behind 21–13 win.

Playing in the first game at brand-new Sanford Stadium (original capacity: 30,000), the Bulldogs of the South were stronger. Georgia's defensive line pummeled Yale, as Booth failed to find breathing room. On one occasion "Catfish" Smith tackled Booth so forcefully that Booth said, "Look here, Smith, there are some things that don't go in this game!"

To that, Smith replied, "I know it, and one of them is Albie Booth."

Heisman Trophy winner Johnny Manziel made Texas A&M and Alabama's first SEC meeting an unforgettable one in 2012. We'll feature that matchup and more in this section of "The Classics," which covers the games forever etched in conference lore.

Perhaps the most memorable part of the day came after the 15–0 Georgia victory. Yale was ready to get out of town, but its locomotive jumped the track and lost electrical power. Players and coaches fumbled around in darkness as onlookers tried to rectify the situation.

Per John D. McCallum: "Finally, a New Haven railroad executive showed them how to do it. It was the only victory scored by the North that day."

1934 LSU @ VANDERBILT

Few politicians have ever supported their SEC team like Louisiana's Huey P. Long. The state governor from 1928 to 1932 and then a US senator until his assassination three years later, Long was a champion of the little guy; he hated the New Deal, supported wealth-sharing programs, and oversaw major infrastructure spending.

He had another controversial platform: building LSU into a powerhouse institution.

Louisiana State University was a regional afterthought until Long assumed governorship. As part of his spending plan, he tripled LSU in size and began construction on its medical school. Football was his marketing tool; he grew the marching band from 28 to 125 members and helped shape the gridiron product by calling plays, giving halftime speeches, and handling some recruiting duties.

When LSU was preparing for a trip to Nashville in 1934, Long made a generous offer to students: he would "borrow" them money for their travel expenses ($7 each). This attracted a horde of takers, with the Associated Press reporting that Long's "bounty is providing transportation of practically the entire Louisiana State University cheering section to Nashville."

Long, known as "the Kingfish," insisted on bringing Louisiana state police to protect the thousands of fans making their way north. The Tennessee Game and Fish Commission declared that the officers could enter the state as "deputy game wardens" to protect whatever "wildlife you may see fit." In all, there were 5,000 LSU students and 1,500 ROTC students, and they marched through the streets of Nashville alongside the band at 9 a.m. on the day of the game. The spectacle prompted the *Nashville Banner* to report, "NASHVILLE SURRENDERS TO HUEY LONG."

U.S. senator Huey Long leads Tigers fans on a parade through Nashville in 1934. Known as the "Kingfish," Long brought thousands of fans with him for LSU's win against Vanderbilt. AP PHOTO

The senator delivered a pregame speech to the crowd that was broadcast to a national audience. The country had anticipated that Long would announce his candidacy for the 1936 presidential election. Instead, he used the moment to predict an LSU victory.

He was right. Vanderbilt, still a powerhouse under the guidance of Dan McGugin, folded in front of the raucous crowd. The Commodores fell, 29–0, marking their worst loss in more than a decade. Louisiana State surged to the forefront of southern football, winning the SEC in 1935 and 1936 and making three consecutive Sugar Bowl trips (all losses) after the 1935–1937 seasons.

Long never made his bid for the presidency. He was shot in the state capitol by the relative of a political opponent in 1935. "The Kingfish" died two days later, but his legacy still lives on at Tigers football games, when the band plays a song he wrote—"Touchdown for LSU"—before kickoff.

1951 SUGAR BOWL: KENTUCKY VS. OKLAHOMA

Much is made of Bear Bryant's impact on the Kentucky football program, and rightfully so; but he shares a hefty amount of the credit with his best quarterback, Vito "Babe" Parilli.

The Rochester, Pennsylvania, native played fullback in high school, then transitioned to quarterback upon arriving in Lexington in 1948. Parilli—a master of Bryant's T formation offense—was so good at ball fakes that he earned the name "Houdini Hands," and he also developed a reputation for burning defenses in the passing game.

In three varsity seasons with Kentucky, Parilli set NCAA career records for completions (331), passing yards (4,351), and passing touchdowns (50). His most memorable season came in 1950, when the Wildcats raced out to a 10–0 record and a No. 2 national ranking.

Bear Bryant speaks with Kentucky halfback Wilbur Jamerson after the 1951 Sugar Bowl. The win capped Kentucky's near-perfect season, which still stands as the best in school history. AP PHOTO

Were it not for a snowy 7–0 loss in the regular season finale at Tennessee, Kentucky might have completed its first—and only—undefeated season. As it happened, the Wildcats still won their first SEC title and received a doozy of a postseason assignment: No. 1 Oklahoma in the Sugar Bowl. At the time, the Sooners had won 31 consecutive games and had just been awarded the national title by both major polls.

Behind two touchdowns from Wilbur Jamerson (including a scoring toss from Parilli), the Wildcats grabbed a 13–0 lead to stun their favored opponents. At the half Bryant gave his star quarterback some odd instructions: Stop throwing the ball. Let the defense finish this off.

"That's how confident he was against Oklahoma," Parilli said. "And he was right."

Kentucky held Oklahoma to a lone second-half touchdown and intercepted a final desperation heave to seal the biggest win in program history. Parilli played one more season before graduating and Bryant coached three more before leaving for Texas A&M. But they couldn't recapture the magic of 1950, and the program is still chasing it nearly seven decades later.

1959 OLE MISS @ LSU

Hated rivals LSU and Ole Miss met for an early version of "the Game of the Century" in 1959. The No. 1-ranked Tigers and No. 3-ranked Rebels convened on Halloween in Baton Rouge, and tickets ran north of $100. One man offered a used Cadillac for four seats. Another—with tongue in cheek, hopefully—offered his wife.

Heisman Trophy favorite Billy Cannon was LSU's primary weapon, but he was unable to get comfortable early. He lost a fumble and his teammates lost two more before the end of the first half. Thanks to the Tigers' suffocating defense, LSU was down only 3–0 at halftime.

Ole Miss, apparently content with its miniscule lead, adopted a frustratingly conservative game plan in the third quarter. Three times, the Rebels punted on *first down*. When they opted to run plays, they went nowhere. Cannon intercepted an errant pass, but LSU's Wendell Harris missed the ensuing 48-yard field goal attempt.

LEGEND
BILLY CANNON

Born in Philadelphia, Mississippi, and raised in Baton Rouge, Louisiana, Billy Cannon didn't need to give much thought to his college decision. His older brother had played football at LSU, and his father worked in the dormitories as a janitor. So, when the rest of the country came calling for his five-star services on the football field, Cannon rebuffed out-of-state suitors in favor of his hometown team.

In nearly every recollection of Cannon's athleticism, it's noted that he ran a 9.5-second 100-yard dash (some say 9.4). He had the speed to outrun defenses, but he often preferred to bulldoze them with his superior strength. It was a mostly unstoppable combination that helped LSU capture the 1958 national title and vaulted Cannon to the 1959 Heisman Trophy. During his legendary Halloween punt return vs. Ole Miss in '59, he evaded eight defenders with that thunder-and-lightning blend.

Following college, he spurned the NFL—which drafted him No. 1 overall—for the newly formed AFL, signing a pro contract with the Houston Oilers to become the first $100,000 player in football history. Over the course of an 11-year career, Cannon won three AFL championships and was a two-time All-Star.

Away from football, he attended dental school during his playing days and became an orthodontist in Baton Rouge after retiring. His post-football life was interrupted, however, by a 30-month stint at a federal correctional institution in Texarkana for possession of $6 million in counterfeit money.

Released in 1986, Cannon began rebuilding his image in the mid-'90s by running the medical program for inmates in the Louisiana State Penitentiary. Redemption stories from the *New York Times* and ESPN's *Outside the Lines* helped Cannon regain trust with the sports world.

"My old daddy had a saying," he said in the latter feature. "It's not how high the peak or how low the valley. It's how far across this valley we're in."

Louisiana State was losing hope in the final quarter when Ole Miss lined up for another punt. What happened next became legendary.

In the words of former *Shreveport Times* editor Jack Fiser: "After three quarters of the most grueling, dead-serious gridding ever seen on this historic sod, there was little left to lift the spirits of LSU partisans or dampen those of the visiting Mississippians. But those Bengals, true to their tradition of fourth-period brilliance, had the last growl."

Cannon misplayed the punt, then collected it on the bounce at his own 11-yard line. He juked around one man, split a pair of defenders, split a *trio* of defenders—in Fiser's words, Cannon "shook numerous Confederates off his anatomy"—ran past two more Rebels, and was soon sprinting all alone down the right sideline.

The touchdown dash gave LSU a 7–3 lead and—following a goal-line stand by the Tigers D, including a game-saving tackle by Cannon—its 19th consecutive win.

It also became the most iconic moment in LSU sports history, and was more than enough to rocket Cannon past all other challengers for the 1959 Heisman Trophy. Ole Miss, however, would soon have its revenge. (We'll get to that later.)

1962 ALABAMA @ GEORGIA TECH

Alabama and Georgia Tech's violent rivalry reached the peak of its infamy in 1961. Alabama had signaled for a fair catch on a punt return, allowing Tech tackler Chick Graning to let down his guard. 'Bama blocker Darwin Holt, sensing weakness, smashed Graning in the face with his left elbow and forearm. The damage: five missing teeth, facial fractures, a broken nose, a sinus fracture, damage to the bone beneath the right eye, a potential skull fracture, and—naturally—a concussion.

Georgia Tech fans were infuriated, but not surprised. They called it characteristic of Alabama football. Bobby Dodd announced that the teams would not play again after the final contractually obligated game in 1964.

All of that made the 1962 Alabama-Georgia Tech game must-see TV. Amidst a nationwide trend of dirty play ("We teach our boys to spear and gore," Ohio State coach Woody Hayes said that year), many expected an uncivilized contest as Tech attempted to keep No. 1-ranked

Bobby Dodd celebrates with his Georgia Tech team following a win vs. No. 1–ranked Alabama in 1962. The game was one of the last between the old SEC rivals, as the annual series was discontinued following Tech's departure from the conference in 1964. GEORGIA TECH ATHLETICS ARCHIVE

'Bama—undefeated in 26 consecutive games—from clinching another SEC championship.

To the surprise of a record crowd at Atlanta's Grant Field, the Jackets and Tide stayed clean. The teams combined for only 30 penalty yards and kept unnecessary physicality to a minimum.

Paul "Bear" Bryant had prepared a bigger surprise than that, though: a pass-happy game plan featuring young quarterback Joe Namath.

The Alabama coach shocked spectators by calling a shotgun formation from his own 23-yard line to open the game. Namath threw it on that play, and the Tide threw it more than three dozen more times on the day. Alabama's 38 total pass attempts kept fans enthralled throughout the contest.

Problem was, Georgia Tech intercepted four of them.

Late in the game, the Crimson Tide was in great position to kick a game-winning field goal and keep its undefeated streak alive. But the suddenly pass-happy Bryant called for another throw, and Namath's final attempt of the day deflected off his receiver and into the hands of Tech defender Don Toner. Georgia Tech had won, 7–6, and Bryant was crushed.

"It was a bad call," he told reporters. "We were close enough to kick. If I had it to go over again I would run two plays through the line and then kick the field goal."

Dodd called it the greatest victory of his career, and—patronizingly— remarked to Bryant that it was the cleanest game he'd ever seen. Others thought so, too, and, in hindsight, the contest marked a turning point for athlete safety in the SEC.

"Bryant may not feel that way after he has reflected on the ruin of his undefeated season, but perhaps Old Bear will be big enough to appreciate himself and what he has done," *Sports Illustrated*'s Morton Sharnick wrote. "And perhaps other coaches will follow his lead, remembering that football is properly a game of skill rather than of savagery."

1966 AUBURN @ FLORIDA

Nearly a quarter century before Steve Spurrier began coaching at Florida, he began laying the foundation for a national-championship program. In October 1966 the senior from Johnson City, Tennessee, dragged the Gators toward their first major bowl appearance—not with his throwing arm, but with his kicking foot.

In the homecoming game, Florida dominated Auburn at the line of scrimmage; the visitors tallied only 158 yards of total offense on the night. Unfortunately, the Gators kept allowing fluky touchdowns. Auburn scored on a 91-yard fumble return and an 89-yard kick return to earn a 20–20 stalemate in the fourth quarter.

Spurrier led a 71-yard drive to take back the lead, but the Tigers offense—led by quarterback Larry Blakeney—finally came to life and responded with a touchdown drive of its own.

Entering the game, Spurrier had been neck and neck in the Heisman Trophy race with Purdue quarterback Bob Griese (who would later lead the Miami Dolphins to the only perfect season in modern NFL history). Heisman ballots had been mailed to voters the week before Florida vs. Auburn, and they were due back one week after the contest.

The Gators quarterback had performed admirably, completing 27 of 40 passes for 259 yards and a touchdown. He also ran for a touchdown and punted the ball seven times for a 46.9-yard average.

But it was not until his final play that he forced voters' hands. In a 27–27 game, Florida faced fourth down from the Auburn 23-yard line with a little more than two minutes remaining.

Gators coach Ray Graves considered inserting Wayne Barfield for the 40-yard attempt, but Barfield had never kicked from that far in a game. Long-range kicking was typically Spurrier's job, though he hadn't made such a kick since the first game of the season. There was no easy choice, so Spurrier essentially made the decision for Graves.

The quarterback laced up his kicking shoe and told Graves to let him "give it a shot." The hold was poor—laces in—but Spurrier smashed the ball down the middle and gave Florida a 30–27 win in front of a press box of national sportswriters.

"You know, I think Spurrier planned that field goal," Graves said afterward. "Anything to give me more gray hair."

In 1991, the year he coached Florida to its first SEC title, Spurrier revealed that he still had the game-winning Spalding J54 football in his personal trophy case. Next to it: the Heisman Trophy.

1969 ALABAMA @ OLE MISS

As the '60s came to a close, college football was no match for *The Lawrence Welk Show*. ABC's Saturday-night variety program featured wholesome music and dancing for viewers across America. When ABC Sports requested that Welk bump his show to an earlier time to make room for a football game, the world-famous band leader refused.

So, on October 4, Alabama and Ole Miss kicked off just before 9 p.m. local time at Birmingham's Legion Field. America didn't know it, but it was about to say hello to a new legend.

Archie Manning, a junior quarterback at Mississippi, was in the midst of an all-time great SEC season. His Rebels weren't particularly

LEGEND
STEVE SPURRIER

Born Steven Orr Spurrier in Miami Beach, the man known to many as "Head Ball Coach" brought the University of Florida football program its first Heisman Trophy, conference title, and national title. And he did it over the course of two Hall of Fame careers.

Spurrier's journey to stardom began at 11 years old, when his father—a preacher—moved the family to Johnson City, Tennessee, where a new congregation (and prominent football program) awaited.

By the time Spurrier entered his final year at Science Hill High School, he was a can't-miss quarterback prospect who had the attention of every major program in the South.

Bear Bryant and Alabama came calling, but the Crimson Tide did not jibe with Spurrier's personal philosophy. He and his father had always rooted for the underdog; 'Bama was the antithesis. So, the hotshot picked a school "that hadn't done much," where he could see early playing time and get in plenty of golf: Florida.

Appearances in the Sugar Bowl and Orange Bowl—Florida's first in each—followed, as did the Heisman and a reputation for theatrics.

"Blindfolded, with his back to the wall, with his hands tied behind him," the *Atlanta Journal*'s John Logue wrote in 1966, "Steve Spurrier would still be a two-point favorite at his own execution."

Following an underwhelming NFL career, Spurrier began coaching and eventually became the head man at Duke in 1987. After twice winning ACC Coach of the Year honors, he became head coach of his alma mater in 1990. At the time, the Gators were on probation for recruiting violations and had never won an SEC title in their eight-decades-plus of existence.

Spurrier guided the Gators to five conference championships and the 1996 national title in his first seven seasons. His "Fun 'n' Gun" offense lit up the SEC, a conference still addicted to run-oriented schemes that moved at the pace of molasses.

He became known for his one-liners. Florida State's "FSU" acronym stood for "Free Shoes University." Tennessee's mediocrity made sense because "you can't spell 'Citrus' [Bowl] without 'UT.'" Auburn's library fire that destroyed 20 books was a "tragedy" because "15 hadn't been colored yet."

He had plenty of cred to back up his wiseass comments, but Spurrier's football life was not without failure. He quarterbacked the Tampa Bay Buccaneers to a 0–14 record and later bombed an opportunity to coach the Washington Redskins, going 12–20 as the highest-paid coach

in NFL history. But he did much more winning than he did losing, with his final act coming at the University of South Carolina from 2005 to 2015.

Traditionally a cellar dweller, USC had never won 11 games in a season. Spurrier did so three years in a row, including an upset of No. 1 Alabama and an SEC East title in 2010.

Never one to bore his audience, Spurrier abruptly retired in the middle of the 2015 season, holding a brief press conference to say good-bye to shocked fans and reporters.

"When something is inevitable, you do it right then," the 70-year-old said. "You don't wait a week or two. This has to happen, so let's do it."

LEGEND
ARCHIE MANNING

The summer before Drew, Mississippi, native Archie Manning won SEC Player of the Year in 1969, his father committed suicide. Manning was the first to find him, and the resulting trauma was enough to make him consider quitting football and getting a job to support his family.

His mother encouraged him to keep playing, so he returned to Oxford in August to prepare for his junior season. Whatever pain or anger he held within did not show on the field. Manning had one of the most impressive seasons in the history of the conference, rushing and passing for a combined 2,264 yards and 23 touchdowns. In one game vs. Alabama—the first prime-time college-football broadcast in history—he posted 540 combined yards, an obscene total even by today's standards.

It's fitting that the Rebels lost that game, because Manning's illustrious career is pockmarked with defeat. He was, in some ways, the captain of the damned, doing his best to make below-average teams win games they had no business winning.

His No. 18 uniform is retired at Ole Miss, and the university put up several "18 mph" signs around campus roads, despite the fact that he never won a conference title. The New Orleans Saints stopped issuing his No. 8 uniform and inducted him into their Ring of Honor despite the fact that he never had a winning record in 10 seasons.

Manning has seemingly been invited to more Hall of Fame inductions and awards ceremonies than just about any other southern football player, and he really never won a damn thing that mattered much at the college or pro level.

It's a testament to how special an athlete he was that he became legendary under those circumstances. His greatness made the win column obsolete in Oxford; it shone through the paper bags embarrassed Saints fans wore over their heads in the '70s.

Family is a major part of Manning's legacy. He met his wife, Olivia, at Ole Miss. His oldest son, Cooper, signed to play receiver at Ole Miss before a spinal condition ended his playing career; he's now a wealthy energy investor. The youngest sons, Peyton and Eli, both became Super Bowl–winning quarterbacks. They are the First Family of football, and it's because Manning, the patriarch, stepped back on the field after losing his own father in 1969.

"You know I thought about him a lot," Manning said in ESPN's acclaimed 2013 documentary *Book of Manning*. "How much he would have enjoyed that. We had some huge wins, some exciting games, and probably the best year I ever had in football—the fall of 1969. You know I wish he could have seen that."

impressive, but he was making defenses look foolish with a mesmerizing scrambling style and his rocket arm.

In the words of Alabama quarterback Scott Hunter, Manning "did everything but bring the popcorn."

Entering the game, no major-college player had ever passed for 300 yards and rushed for 100 yards in the same contest. Manning obliterated the standard. He passed for 436 and ran for 104 as the Rebels pushed the tempo in front of a national audience.

He threw a pair of touchdowns and ran for three more scores while Hunter and the Alabama offense countered with scoring drives of their own. In all, the teams combined for 65 points and nearly 1,100 yards. Veteran coaches Bear Bryant and Johnny Vaught were beside themselves with shame.

"I was in a room with them, him and Coach Vaught, one time at a function," Manning said in 2015. "And somebody came in and said, 'That had to be one of the greatest games y'all have ever had.' And almost simultaneously they said, 'That was the worst [expletive] game I ever coached in my life.' They weren't proud of it."

The supposed embarrassment made for excellent TV. With time winding down, Hunter—who finished with 300 yards passing—hit George Ranager on a fourth-and-goal play to win the game, 33–32.

In the nearly five decades that have since passed, Hunter's heroics have paled next to Manning's coming-out party.

"I think he really made the game," Hunter said. "I was more a drop-back passer and we ran a pro-style offense. I was handing the ball off to Johnny Musso and throwing to great receivers. Archie was like a circus performer. He was the whole show."

1982 ALABAMA @ TENNESSEE

The legacies of Bear Bryant and Nick Saban have plenty in common. For instance, both Alabama coaches turned the storied "Third Saturday in October" rivalry between the Crimson Tide and Volunteers into a joke.

Just as Saban has now won 11 straight wins against the Volunteers (2007–2017), Bryant did so between 1971 and 1981. In his final season at Alabama, the Bear's Crimson Tide was undefeated and ranked No. 2 when they attempted to make it a dozen.

Unranked Tennessee had plenty of talent—including future NFL Hall of Fame defensive lineman Reggie White and future Super Bowl champion receiver Willie Gault—but was a 14-point underdog. Coach Johnny Majors decided to break out all-orange uniforms for the occasion, and 95,342 fans arrived at Neyland Stadium to see if the Vols could halt the ugly skid.

In the first half, Tennessee seemed to say "nope." The Vols fell behind, 14–3, as quarterback Alan Cockrell tossed three interceptions. The two sides traded scores to make it 21–13, Alabama, at the end of the second quarter.

From there, White and the oft-maligned Tennessee defense locked up the Tide, and the Vols O began rolling. Cockrell found Mike Miller for a 39-yard touchdown in the third quarter, and then halfback Chuck Coleman powered a 90-yard scoring drive capped by a 34-yard touchdown run to make it 35–21, Volunteers, in the fourth with about seven minutes left.

Neyland Stadium was anxious to run out the clock, and rightfully so. Alabama struck back with a 79-yard touchdown drive, and then got the ball back with a final chance to tie or win.

A national championship season was on the line for 'Bama when quarterback Walter Lewis tossed a pass from the Tennessee 27-yard line into the back of the end zone. Tennessee defensive back Lee Jenkins leapt toward the ball, then everything went black as he careened into another player.

"The next thing I heard was the roar from the crowd," Jenkins said, "but I didn't know if Alabama had scored or not."

It hadn't. Jenkins had tipped the ball toward teammate Mike Terry, who caught it in the end zone for the game-clinching—and streak-busting—interception. After the final second ticked off, Tennessee fans stormed the turf and tore down the goalposts in celebration.

Few realized it was Bryant's final visit to Knoxville. The Alabama legend would retire following the season and suffer a fatal heart attack in January. The Volunteers seemed to understand the importance of the win,

LEGEND
REGGIE WHITE

Reggie White was always bigger than the other kids, from the time he was born to the time he graduated from the University of Tennessee. For the most part, that was a good thing. But elementary school was an exception.

Peers called him "Bigfoot" and referenced the 1960s TV show *Land of the Giants*. White's awkward phase ended with a thud—literally—when he began tackling kids on the gridiron in seventh grade. Soon, the Chattanooga, Tennessee, native promised his mother he would become a professional football player and pay her bills.

He also promised to serve God. The Whites were a conservative Baptist family, and Reggie found the pulpit to be just as fulfilling as the football field.

He destroyed quarterbacks as an All-America defensive end for the Volunteers on Saturdays, and then traveled the state to give sermons as an ordained minister on Sundays. His dual gifts earned him one of football's most famous nicknames: "the Minister of Defense."

White left UT as the Vols' all-time sack leader and decided to sign with the fledgling United States Football League over the NFL. In doing so, he stayed in the Volunteer State to play for the Memphis Showboats. After two seasons, he joined the Philadelphia Eagles and became the NFL's Defensive Rookie of the Year. Following his second season in Philly, White earned the first of 13 consecutive Pro Bowl selections.

In the strike-shortened 1987 season, he recorded 21 sacks in 12 games. He also was a pioneer in the NFL free agency movement, joining a class-action lawsuit against the league and eventually becoming the first major star to sign via that process in 1993. White helped his new franchise—the Green Bay Packers—win its first Super Bowl in nearly three decades in January 1997 (he had a game-record three sacks), and finally stepped away from football four years later with an NFL-record 198 career sacks in tow.

The Minister of Defense suffered a fatal heart attack the day after Christmas in 2004. He was 43 years old.

"I don't know if he's the best," former Packers general manager Ron Wolf said after learning the news. "But it won't take long to call the roll."

regardless. White called it "the best victory we have ever had," and his coach echoed that statement.

"As long as I live, this game will have special meaning," Majors said. "In this time span, it is as great a win as we have ever had at Tennessee."

1988 AUBURN @ LSU ("THE EARTHQUAKE GAME")

On October 8, 1988, Don Stevenson was sitting at home when he heard a loud noise coming from the Louisiana State University campus. The seismologist lived less than a mile from Tiger Stadium, but he didn't realize "Death Valley" was responsible for the din until watching the local news later that night.

The next morning, he was at LSU's geoscience building when student worker Riley Milner brought the previous day's seismograph to Stevenson's office.

"We didn't believe at first, but started looking at it closer," Milner later said. "It was a total surprise."

Back to Saturday night: Louisiana State was locked in a defensive battle with No. 4-ranked Auburn, and the home Tigers had failed to cross midfield for 55 minutes.

When quarterback Tommy Hodson and the LSU offense took the field for their final attempt at victory, they faced a 6–0 deficit and an elite defense that would surrender only 92 points all season. Hodson had been booed and benched early in the game. But with 5:07 remaining, he had an improbable chance at redemption.

The Tigers inched down the field. By the time LSU reached Auburn's 11-yard line, it had moved just 64 yards in 14 plays and faced fourth-and-10. If Auburn made the stop, it would win in Baton Rouge for the first time since 1939.

Louisiana State receiver Eddie Fuller had already blown two major opportunities. He dropped a Hodson pass in the end zone earlier in the game, and then stepped out of bounds as he reeled in another potential score on the final drive. Hodson either didn't notice or didn't care. He took a five-step drop, stood tall, then fired another strike to Fuller in the back of the end zone. This time, the junior caught it.

LSU offensive linemen Ralph Norwood and Robert Packnett raise their hands in celebration after a last-minute win vs. Auburn in 1988. The raucous crowd at Tiger Stadium provoked a seismograph reading at the campus geoscience building. LSU ATHLETICS

Tiger Stadium erupted. David Browndyke drilled the winning extra point, and the LSU defense snuffed out Auburn's last offensive gasp in the final 1:41.

And that was it. A great game, but not a legendary one. At least, not until the seeds were sown on Sunday morning. The seismograph Stevenson and Milner reviewed showed "something unusual": a mass of seismic activity at the same moment Hodson hit Fuller on fourth-and-10.

It clicked. The LSU crowd—by screaming and stomping—had created a miniature earthquake. Stevenson framed the seismograph and taped it to his office window. Accounts differ on how the story eventually reached a national audience, but it's generally agreed upon that ESPN helped popularize it with an "Earthquake Game" segment in the early '90s.

Ever since, the ending has stood alongside Billy Cannon's legendary punt return vs. Ole Miss as one of the greatest moments in LSU football history. There are plenty of skeptics—especially from Auburn—as to the veracity of the earthquake claims, but look no further than the immediate recap by *Montgomery Advertiser* editor Phillip Marshall, who called the scene "berserk" well before anyone mentioned an earthquake.

"You'd have to be here to believe it," he wrote.

1994 LSU @ AUBURN ("THE INTERCEPTION GAME")

Forcing five interceptions in a single game is considered excellent. Forcing five interceptions in the final quarter to keep a 13-game winning streak alive?

"You can't explain it," Auburn coach Terry Bowden said. "You almost want to be humorous, but I think maybe we've seen something historic. I've never been in a game like that. I've never seen one."

Louisiana State quarterback Jamie Howard and the Tigers had a 23–9 lead on No. 11-ranked Auburn with a little more than 12 minutes remaining at Jordan-Hare Stadium. The LSU defense was dominating Auburn, leading many to believe the visiting Tigers would just run the ball to ice the victory.

Bucking the "play it safe" approach, coach Curley Hallman called a pass on third-and-8. Howard tossed an interception to Auburn defensive back Ken Alvis, who returned it for a touchdown—bowling over Howard near the goal line—to cut the deficit to 23–16. One drive later, Fred Smith robbed another errant Howard throw and took it to the house. Tied game.

In an impressive twist, Howard stayed calm and responded with a 13-play, 70-yard drive that netted a go-ahead field goal. Auburn punted on the ensuing drive, and LSU appeared to avoid catastrophe until—you guessed it—Howard dropped back to pass again on third-and-4 from the Auburn 32-yard line.

"I couldn't believe it," Auburn safety Brian Robinson said. "I couldn't believe they were throwing again. But I was glad they did."

A pair of defenders tipped the ball, which landed in Robinson's hands. He shot down the left sideline for a 30–26 Auburn lead.

If that's where it had ended for Howard, perhaps the game would not have achieved the notoriety it did. But it got worse. Louisiana State still had 1:55 remaining, and the Tigers began another drive, this time *needing* to pass to stay alive.

Howard chucked another interception to Robinson at the Auburn 11-yard line. Robinson fumbled the ball back to LSU, giving the road Tigers one final chance, but everyone in the building knew it was for naught. Chris Shelling snagged interception No. 6 of the day—No. 5 of the fourth quarter—in the end zone to seal the victory.

The lifeless Auburn offense, which recorded only 16 yards and one first down in the second half, stood on the sideline, trying to reconcile the doldrums of a terrible performance with the fact that the Tigers were still (somehow) undefeated.

"All I could do is look up at the sky," receiver Frank Sanders said, "and say, 'This can't be happening.'"

1996 AUBURN @ GEORGIA

The first overtime game in SEC history was also the 100th edition of the "Deep South's Oldest Rivalry" between Auburn and Georgia. It *also* happened to feature a game-tying 30-yard touchdown pass with no time remaining in regulation, a miracle play that was quickly overshadowed by four extra periods at Jordan-Hare Stadium.

(All of that without mentioning the now-iconic photograph of Bull-dogs mascot Uga V attempting to bite Auburn wide receiver Robert Baker in the end zone.)

In the aftermath of a 56–49 Georgia victory, newspaper reporters faced a problem: there was too much to write about. Where to begin?

Auburn had built a 28–7 lead, then watched it crumble as Georgia quarterback Mike Bobo helped the Bulldogs come back. Bobo, who began the game on the bench, led a short touchdown drive late in the third quarter to get the Bulldogs within striking distance. In the fourth, he connected with Hines Ward for a 69-yard touchdown and then Corey Allen for a 30-yard score at the final gun.

The latter play was Allen's first career touchdown catch; he fought away Auburn defensive back Jayson Bray to snag the football near the goal line, then reached past Bray for the tying score.

It came after both coaches thought the game was over. Bobo had been sacked with time running out, and the Georgia offense had no chance to get set for another play. In celebration, Auburn defensive tackle Charles

Dorsey picked up the dead football and began running with it. Instead of allowing the clock to run out, the officials stopped it at one second to reclaim the football and spot it correctly.

Auburn coach Terry Bowden had already taken off his headset and begun walking onto the field to shake the hand of Georgia's Jim Donnan, who was also about to shed his headset when he noticed the commotion.

Bobo got one more chance, and history followed.

In overtime both defenses were absolutely powerless against the run. Auburn's Dameyune Craig and Georgia's Robert Edwards traded scores on the ground in the first period. Edwards and Auburn's Fred Beasley did the same in the second. Craig and Edwards were at it again in the third.

When Georgia's Torin Kirtsey powered in from the 1-yard line to open scoring in the fourth period, it was fair to wonder if the near-four-hour game would ever end. It did—barely.

Craig took a shotgun snap on fourth-and-3, charged around the right side of the line, and lunged toward the first down. He came up 1 yard short.

Bulldogs began sprinting around the field. One did a cartwheel. A couple of players picked up coach Jim Donnan and paraded him around. When a small group of Georgia players approached from behind with a Gatorade cooler, they were apparently too tired to lift it high enough to dump it on Donnan; instead, it poured onto the heads of the players carrying the coach.

"You're happy to win but, dang, you're glad it's over because you don't know if you had another one in you," Georgia defensive coordinator Joe Kines said later. "It would have been Sunday preaching, church services fixing to start because we were there all night."

1997 FLORIDA STATE @ FLORIDA

Florida-Florida State was college football's most important rivalry of the 1990s. The schools, separated by roughly 150 miles on Interstate 10, consistently fielded national title contenders (from 1991 to 1998, both teams finished in the Top 10 each season), and the annual November finale between the Seminoles and Gators always had a direct influence on the major-bowl picture.

The hatred reached its peak in 1997, one year after No. 2 Florida State upset No. 1 Florida in Tallahassee, and nearly 11 months after Florida got its revenge—and claimed its first national title—in a Sugar Bowl rematch.

When No. 1-ranked Florida State visited No. 9-ranked Florida on November 22, 1997, the teams met at midfield to shove each other around in pregame warm-ups.

"The fight started then," Gators defensive end Jevon Kearse said, "and it just went on from there."

After kickoff UF coach Steve Spurrier was in his element. He surprised Bobby Bowden and the 'Noles with a two-quarterback rotation that put a different passer behind center on nearly every play. On the opening drive, the Gators ran a double-reverse pass that landed in the arms of quarterback Rob Johnson, who picked up a key fourth-down conversion. Moments later, running back Fred Taylor gashed the Florida State defense for a 3-yard touchdown run.

Taylor, a future Top 10 NFL pick and Pro Bowl running back, boosted his draft stock with 162 yards against the nation's No. 1 rushing defense.

He made two major mistakes in the first half, however. The first came two possessions after his opening score, when he fumbled the ball deep in Gators territory for a Florida State scoop-and-score. Two possessions after that, Taylor caught a short pass and fumbled again, this time setting up a short Sebastian Janikowski field goal for the Seminoles.

With 8:49 remaining in the second quarter, Florida State quarterback Thad Busby found receiver Melvin Pearsall for a 5-yard touchdown pass and a 17–6 lead.

That's when Spurrier's quarterback rotation took hold again. Senior Noah Brindise hit Travis McGriff for a 50-yard completion, then Johnson went back to McGriff for a 5-yard touchdown. On Florida's next drive, Spurrier's offense raced down the field and took an 18–17 lead on another short touchdown run by Taylor.

The back-and-forth continued as Janikowski nailed a go-ahead field goal. Taylor completed his redemption in the third quarter when he broke a 61-yard touchdown to recapture the lead. Florida State's Travis Minor responded with a 10-yard scoring run on the other end, and Janikowski kicked another field goal to extend the lead to 29–25. In celebration, the hefty lefty mocked the famous "Gator Chomp" with his arms.

With 2:38 remaining, Spurrier dug deep into his bag of trick plays, so deep that he made up the play call on the spot and drew it on a laminated sheet. At least two of the receivers had no idea what routes to run. One of them was Jacquez Green, a junior from Fort Valley, Georgia, with more than 100 career catches.

Johnson, the quarterback, noticed Green was lost, so he made a quick pre-snap decision at the line of scrimmage and signaled for Green to run a hitch-and-go.

Florida State cornerback Samari Rolle had seen the double move earlier in the game, but he still bit on the hitch. Green blew by him down the sideline and hauled in a 63-yard completion to the Seminoles' 17-yard line. Taylor followed that with a run to the 1, and then punched in the go-ahead score with 1:50 left.

When FSU began its final drive, the Swamp was roaring.

Spurrier had given Ben Hill Griffin Stadium its ubiquitous nickname in the early '90s, and Florida's home-field advantage quickly became one of the country's most intimidating. Against the Seminoles, it reached a new level.

"Give the legendary Swamp its due," wrote *Tallahassee Democrat* reporter Gerald Ensley. "Its denizens were every bit as loud as advertised. They roared from kickoff to finish, and their din at the end was ear-piercing."

Amidst the noise, Busby threw an interception to Florida linebacker Dwayne Thomas to send Gators fans into delirium. Florida radio man Mick Hubert compared the scene to "an insane asylum."

Everyone knew they'd just witnessed a classic, perhaps the best game ever played in the Swamp.

Brindise, the senior quarterback forced into a two-man rotation, seemed to understand the importance of the moment. He made a simple request of Spurrier as time ran out.

"I asked coach if I could at least take the last snap," he said. "That was really special. I have that ball tucked away in my bag already."

1998 ARKANSAS @ TENNESSEE

On fourth-and-9, Tennessee quarterback Tee Martin saw his favorite receiver, Peerless Price, streaking across the field. He let go of the football, and Neyland Stadium held its breath as the Volunteers' perfect season hung in the balance.

Incomplete. The crowd groaned, and Martin trotted off the field with 1:54 remaining.

Tennessee, the nation's freshly minted No. 1 team, appeared headed for a tragic setback in its quest for a 9–0 start. No. 10-ranked Arkansas had stormed into Neyland Stadium and taken a commanding 21–3 lead in the first half. Quarterback Clint Stoerner was surgical, tossing a trio of touchdowns against one of the strongest defenses in the country.

Martin and the Vols battled back to make it 24–22 late in the fourth, but it seemed for naught when his fourth-and-9 pass fell to the turf.

The Neyland crowd began to accept defeat. Not Martin.

"I felt something strange," Martin said. "If I had thought the game was over, I would've taken off my shoulder pads. But something told me we were going to get the ball back."

On second-and-12 with 1:47 remaining, Stoerner took the snap and began a play-action fake. His foot caught on an offensive lineman's cleat, and he dropped the football as he fell to the ground. Tennessee defensive tackle Billy Ratliff—who had shoved his blocker into Stoerner—fell on the ball, and Martin's inkling proved correct.

Thus began a star-making turn for Vols running back Travis Henry, a sophomore who had received a promotion five weeks earlier when Jamal Lewis suffered a season-ending knee injury.

Henry slashed his way to the Arkansas 28-yard line on first down, and the offensive line opened up a big hole on the left side moments later to spring Henry to the 13. Then, up the middle to the 2. With half a minute remaining, Henry (197 yards on 32 carries) dove over the line of scrimmage for the winning touchdown. The comeback was complete.

Officials from the Fiesta Bowl—which was set to host the first-ever BCS national championship game—were on the field during the final minutes. Tennessee's late reversal of fortune eventually led to an SEC title and a Fiesta bid en route to its first national championship since 1967.

"It was incredible," Phillip Fulmer said. "Sometimes you have to be fortunate, as well as good."

What's the difference between fortunate and lucky?

"There's not a lot of difference," he said. "'Fortunate' just sounds better."

Martin, the star quarterback, disagreed.

"I won't give luck the credit," he said. "I give the credit to God . . . He's standing up there right now with Smokey next to him, wearing an orange jersey."

1999 ALABAMA @ FLORIDA

As the new millennium crept closer, Alabama was reeling. Within the span of two weeks, the Crimson Tide lost to Louisiana Tech, forced out its athletic director, and dealt with incessant hot-seat rumors regarding its head coach.

While that was happening, Mike DuBose and his 'Bama team had to prepare for a trip to the Swamp to face No. 3-ranked Florida. The Tide had not won in Gainesville since 1986. In fact, only one SEC team had come away from the Swamp victorious during the entire decade, and no team from any conference had defeated Florida at home in 30 games.

Steve Spurrier's Gators appeared headed for another championship run when the No. 21-ranked Tide came to town in September.

Alabama surprised everyone with a strong first half, but Florida quickly erased its 13–7 deficit in the third quarter with a pick-six by cornerback Bennie Anderson. A track meet ensued. Alabama raced back the other direction for a 47-yard touchdown pass from Andrew Zow to running back Shaun Alexander. Florida returned the favor with an 80-yard drive that culminated in a short touchdown pass from Doug Johnson to receiver Darrell Jackson.

Jackson finished the afternoon with three touchdowns, but it was Alexander who stole the headlines; Alabama's star running back recorded 200 yards from scrimmage and found the end zone four times while getting roughed up by the Florida defense.

"I got punched a couple of times," he said. "They knocked my helmet off on one play, and I bit my lip. It's a physical game. That's why football is so awesome. Not a lot of people can play it."

Alabama running back Shaun Alexander points skyward after a touchdown against Florida in 1999. His 200 yards from scrimmage helped 'Bama win at The Swamp for the first time in 13 years. AP PHOTO/DON FRAZIER

The fifth-year senior from Florence, Kentucky, had only two scores to his name when 'Bama, down 33–26, punted the ball away with 3:20 remaining. Jackson, normally a sure-handed return man, muffed the kick and the Crimson Tide began a shortened quest for the tying touchdown.

LONGEST HOME WINNING STREAKS IN THE SAME STADIUM, SEC HISTORY

Alabama, 57 (1963–1982 at Denny Stadium)—Lost to Southern Miss, 38–29

Tennessee, 30 (1928–1933 at Neyland Stadium)—Lost to Alabama, 12–6. The team competed in the Southern Conference during the first five seasons of its streak

Auburn, 30 (1952–1961 at Cliff Hare Stadium)—Lost to Kentucky, 14–12

Florida, 30 (1994–1999 at Ben Hill Griffin Stadium)—Lost to Alabama, 40–39 (OT)

Ole Miss, 24 (1952–1960 at Hemingway Stadium)—Tied LSU, 6–6. Ripped off 13 more wins before losing to Mississippi State, 17–20, in 1964

Georgia, 24 (1980–1983 at Sanford Stadium)—Lost to Auburn, 13–7

Florida, 23 (1990–1993 at Ben Hill Griffin Stadium)—Lost to Florida State, 33–21

LSU, 22 (2009–2012 at Tiger Stadium)—Lost to Alabama, 21–17

Alabama, 20 (1941–1942, 1944–1951 at Denny Stadium)—Lost to Villanova, 41–18

Alabama, 20 (2008–2010 at Bryant-Denny Stadium)—Lost to Auburn, 28–27

On fourth-and-2 from the 13-yard line, Alexander slipped past a defender at the line of scrimmage, plowed through a defensive back, and high-stepped into the end zone.

In overtime Florida's Johnson found Reche Caldwell on third-and-4 for the go-ahead score, and the Swamp reached a fever pitch until Jeff Chandler biffed the extra-point attempt past the right upright.

The Gators had suddenly lost their momentum, and it showed. The Crimson Tide ran a counter to the left on its first play; Alexander slipped two tackles and raced into the end zone, where he purposefully collapsed to the turf so teammates could pile on top of him.

All kicker Chris Kemp had to do was kick the extra point and Alabama would get the W.

Born in Gainesville and raised in Jacksonville, the walk-on junior said afterward that he was "too relaxed" before the kick. He pushed his attempt too far the right, a carbon copy of Chandler's error.

The kicker slumped his shoulders and trotted back to the sideline. Griffin Stadium went wild as double overtime appeared imminent.

But this Florida celebration was cut short, too; there was a flag on the field. The Gators had jumped offside in an attempt to block the kick. Kemp got a redo, and he once again failed to hit the ball cleanly. The pigskin sailed left as it reached the goalpost, and fans were unsure of its fate until one of the referees shot his hands to the sky.

Despite giving up 39 points in a venue it had not conquered in 13 years, Alabama emerged victorious.

2001 GEORGIA @ TENNESSEE ("THE HOBNAIL BOOT")

Legendary college football moments tend to generate nicknames, ranging from vague ("the Play") to specific ("the Bush Push"). In most cases, those designations arrived in the hours and days afterward, when reporters were suddenly struck with inspiration.

If Georgia played a classic game, though, you simply needed to rewind Larry Munson's broadcast.

Munson, the school's radio play-by-play man, served up several memorable calls between 1966 and 2008. He introduced Herschel Walker to the nation ("My God, a freshman!") and cheered on Lindsay Scott's

Former Georgia play-by-play announcer Larry Munson made a handful of legendary calls in his career. Perhaps none are more ingrained in Georgia lore than "The Hobnail Boot." A sample: "This is a sweet, golden, ungodly, unbelievable miracle we have pulled." AP PHOTO/*ATHENS BANNER-HERALD*

miracle touchdown against Florida ("Run, Lindsay!"), among other iconic moments.

Perhaps his greatest call came at Tennessee's Neyland Stadium in 2001. After the No. 6-ranked Volunteers scored a go-ahead touchdown with 44 seconds remaining—a 62-yard screen pass to running back Travis Stephens—Munson was heartbroken. He complained about the unranked Bulldogs' missed opportunities and seemed to think a tragic loss was imminent.

Mark Richt was coaching his first SEC road game, and the 'Dawgs had not won in Knoxville since Walker's famous demolition of Bill Bates in 1980. Few expected any late fireworks.

Tennessee decided to go with a squib kickoff, and it backfired. Georgia tight end Randy McMichael snared it around the 35-yard line and brought it to the 40. Quarterback David Greene coolly led the Bulldogs down the field, finding McMichael on two key plays as Georgia reached the Tennessee 6-yard line. Then, the fateful play call came in: "P-44 Haynes."

Fullback Verron Haynes slipped through the line as Greene faked a handoff to running back Musa Smith. The linebackers caved toward Smith, then Greene lofted an easy touchdown pass over their heads to Haynes.

Only nine seconds remained. Munson was beside himself.

"My God Almighty, did you see what he did?" Munson exclaimed. "David Greene just straightened up and we snuck the fullback over! We just dumped it over! 26–24! We just stepped on their face with a hobnail boot and broke their nose! We just crushed their face!"

He wasn't done.

"This is a sweet, golden, ungodly, unbelievable miracle we have pulled," Munson said. "They broke our hearts, and we just came back down the field."

Richt had his first road win, and he was off to a record-setting tenure in Athens that included a pair of SEC championships. A decade later, when he looked back at that signature win over Tennessee, he gave credit to one man in the press box.

"It was awesome, because it was a great victory," Richt said, "but to have Larry Munson, who is legendary already, to have one of his calls of a game that I was involved in is very meaningful to me."

2001 ARKANSAS @ OLE MISS

There was nothing special about the first 60 minutes of football between these two unranked teams. A non-sellout crowd showed up to watch Ole Miss host Arkansas, and it got a fairly pedestrian four quarters that resulted in a 17–17 tie at the end of regulation.

Rebels quarterback Eli Manning was the big name involved; few other players on the field had any national recognition at that point.

Not even the novelty of overtime was much of a selling point. Since the new rules had been implemented five years earlier, both schools had played into extra periods multiple times. Arkansas was 2–0 in such games, while Ole Miss was 5–2.

The odds were stacked against a legendary finish, let alone one that people would remember a week later.

The marathon began as a short sprint. Arkansas's Cedric Cobbs raced in from 16 yards out for the first score. The Arkansas sideline erupted, sensing victory. But Manning responded with an 11-yard bullet to Jason Armstead. Minutes later, Ole Miss fans groaned when Manning fumbled away the ball; Arkansas just needed a field goal to win. Of course, Razorbacks kicker Brennan O'Donohoe pushed his attempt too far to the right, and the teams went to a third overtime.

Hogs quarterback Matt Jones struck on the first play, taking a keeper 25 yards to the end zone (the 2-point conversion attempt failed). The Rebels struck back with a 1-yard run by Joe Gunn (the 2-point conversion attempt also failed). The teams traded 20-plus-yard touchdowns in the fourth overtime, but once again whiffed on both 2-point tries. A pair of four-play touchdown drives—and two more failed conversions—in the fifth period could not break the deadlock, either.

"During the third and fourth overtimes, I was thinking let's just blow the whistle and say, 'Boys, let's just go to the house,'" Ole Miss coach David Cutcliffe said afterward.

Manning hit tight end Doug Zeigler for a sixth-period touchdown and (finally) converted the 2-pointer. Problem was, Arkansas matched it with 8 points of its own, including a wild 2-point conversion toss from Jones to defensive end-turned-tight end Jason Peters.

Entering the seventh overtime, the scoreboard read Ole Miss 50, Arkansas 50. No college football teams had ever played a longer game. The schools had combined to score 66 points in extra time, and they were about to add more.

Arkansas running back Mark Pierce plunged in for a 1-yard score and Jones hit DeCori Birmingham for an extra 2 points. Manning matched the touchdown with a beautiful arcing throw to Armstead in the corner of the end zone.

One play remained. Ole Miss lined up on the left hash mark, 3 yards from an eighth overtime. Jones couldn't watch; he kneeled and stared at the grass on the Arkansas sideline. Manning motioned flanker Jamie Armstrong toward the offensive line, took the snap, then made a decisive throw over the middle to Zeigler. It connected, but Arkansas senior linebacker Jermaine Petty flew in to stuff him short of the goal line.

The highest-scoring game in SEC history was finally over. Arkansas 58, Ole Miss 56.

"There really wasn't a loser," said Manning, who finished with a school-record six touchdown passes. "We just came up short."

2001 TENNESSEE @ FLORIDA

Turns out, "the Hobnail Boot" couldn't puncture Tennessee's national title hopes. The Volunteers rebounded from that September loss to Georgia by winning six in a row. Ranked No. 5 in the country, they headed down to Gainesville for a heavily hyped matchup with the No. 2-ranked Florida Gators.

Tennessee defensive lineman John Henderson sacks Florida quarterback Rex Grossman during a win in 2001. Florida had not lost to Tennessee at home in three decades. AP PHOTO/SCOTT AUDETTE

(The tragic events of September 11 had led to major schedule revisions; Florida-Tennessee was now the regular-season finale, and the conference title game would be played the second weekend of December.)

As far as Top 5 matchups go, this one was unusually one-sided. Florida had not lost to Tennessee at home in 30 years, and Steve Spurrier's red-hot Gators were favored by 18 points after defeating their previous six SEC opponents by an average of 37.3. From their hotel rooms, Volunteers players watched ESPN's *College GameDay* experts predict an easy win for the home team.

"They gave us no chance at all," running back Travis Stephens said a decade later. "Once they did that, it was like the hotel erupted. . . . Everybody just ran around screaming in the halls."

In the locker room before the game, Vols coach Phillip Fulmer told his players a story: He had played on the last Tennessee team to beat Florida in Gainesville. Back in 1971, he was a guard when the Vols offense drove 99 yards for a go-ahead score.

"Those guys put the same jocks on you do," Fulmer said. "Those guys like the same girls you guys like. Everything's the same."

His team believed it and raced out to a 14–0 lead in the first quarter. The advantage wouldn't last long, though; Florida quarterback Rex Grossman was in the midst of one of the best passing seasons in school history, and he led four scoring drives in the second quarter to give the Gators a 20–14 halftime lead. It seemed the analysts and oddsmakers could breathe easy; Florida was headed for another SEC East title.

But Tennessee had an unstoppable All-American of its own: Stephens. The running back darted 35 yards for a third-quarter score to take back the lead. Grossman and the Gators went back the other way, with the sophomore quarterback making a seemingly impossible completion on fourth-and-5 to keep possession and allow Jeff Chandler to drill his third field goal of the day.

From there, two key moments defined the game: First, Tennessee converted a fourth-and-1 near midfield with 14:22 remaining that led to another go-ahead touchdown.

Second, Grossman and the Gators—down 34–26—scored a touchdown with 1:10 remaining and lined up for the tying 2-point conversion.

Grossman took a shotgun snap, looked to his left, danced around the pocket, and then fired left toward Jabar Gaffney. The ball fell incomplete, and Gaffney immediately screamed at the official for a pass interference flag.

Spurrier, too, was adamant that pass interference should have been called on Tennessee's Buck Fitzgerald. Fulmer essentially admitted as much, saying, "It kind of makes up for one in Knoxville [in 2000] where Gaffney dropped the ball and official called it a touchdown."

The call did not change, and Tennessee had completed a massive upset. The Vols were headed to Atlanta for an SEC championship game vs. LSU and a potential Rose Bowl berth in the BCS national championship game. (They would lose to Nick Saban's Tigers at the Georgia Dome and miss out on another national title.)

Though it wasn't known at the time, Spurrier had coached his final game at the Swamp; he would sign with the NFL's Washington Redskins during the off-season.

Stephens, who had patiently waited his turn behind Vols running backs Jamal Lewis and Travis Henry, finished with 226 yards—the second most by any player against Florida—and two touchdowns on just 19 carries. Without him, the Vols would not have ended their 30-year turmoil at the Swamp.

"We've always known we had the artillery to do this," Stephens said afterward. "We just had to go do it. We're over that hump."

2003 ARKANSAS @ KENTUCKY

This one didn't need seven overtime periods to get the blood pumping. Kentucky and Arkansas put on an electric four quarters that featured a pair of blocked punts returned for touchdowns, several 30-plus-yard plays, and a tying touchdown pass to make it 24–24 with 1:38 remaining.

When the final seconds of regulation slipped away, the ESPN broadcast team knew it might be a long night. The network referenced Arkansas's seven-overtime victory against Ole Miss in 2001 and its six-overtime loss to Tennessee in 2002. Could the Razorbacks turn in another marathon classic?

Yep.

Quarterback Matt Jones—the star of that 2001 game—led a short touchdown drive to open the extra period. Kentucky's Jared Lorenzen matched it. Ditto in the second period.

Kentucky had an excellent chance to win in the third when it held Arkansas to a field goal and then drove to the 1-yard line to set up a dramatic fourth-and-goal. Coach Rich Brooks, worried about his team's depth, kept his offense on the field to decide the game one way or another. But an illegal substitution resulted in a 5-yard penalty and a field goal, allowing the madness to continue.

Both quarterbacks ran for touchdowns in the fourth period and connected on 2-point conversion opportunities. Minutes later, they both found the end zone again—Jones on a pass, Lorenzen on a rush—but failed the conversion attempts.

In the sixth, another chance for UK to win: the 'Cats had a 2-point advantage when Jones dropped back for the tying conversion. It appeared as if he would be sacked to end the game, but he pump-faked, slipped away, and hit George Wilson to keep the Hogs alive.

The seventh overtime period finally brought a conclusion. Arkansas wide receiver-turned-running back DeCori Birmingham (career-high 196 rushing yards) ran in from 25 yards out, and the Razorbacks defense eventually stripped Lorenzen of the football on fourth-and-3.

The final: Arkansas 71, Kentucky 63.

After 4 hours and 56 minutes of football, the game ended at 12:01 a.m. local time. The teams had run 202 total plays, totaled 1,111 yards, and scored an NCAA Football Bowl Subdivision record 133 points (the *Louisville Courier-Journal* noted that the Saturday NBA game between the Minnesota Timberwolves and Toronto Raptors yielded only 129).

Much like the 2001 game vs. Ole Miss, Jones had been unbelievable. He accounted for 24 points in overtime alone, constantly eluding Kentucky defenders and firing perfect passes to his receivers. His 372 combined yards and four touchdowns were particularly impressive, considering he didn't enter the game until the second quarter.

His coach, Houston Nutt, now owned victories in the two longest games in NCAA history.

"As long as we get to seven [overtimes]," he said, "it's OK."

2007 FLORIDA @ LSU

If one game solidified Les Miles's legacy as "the Mad Hatter," this was it. Louisiana State was ranked No. 1 in the Associated Press poll for the first time in nearly five decades. Florida was ranked No. 9 and boasted an impressive spread attack run by eventual Heisman Trophy winner Tim Tebow.

It was Tebow and the Gators who jumped out to a 10–0 lead in Death Valley. From there, LSU spent much of the game simply trying to catch up. Such a comeback would have been impossible without Miles dialing up five successful fourth-down conversions, including three in the final quarter.

Here is a breakdown of those crucial moments:

LSU coach Les Miles, aka "The Mad Hatter," pumps his fists in celebration after a narrow win vs. Florida in 2007. Miles dialed up five successful fourth-down conversions during the victory. AP PHOTO/ALEX BRANDON

- **Florida 10, LSU 0: fourth-and-goal from the Florida 1-yard line, 6:08 remaining in the second quarter.** Backup quarterback Ryan Perrilloux ran the double option to his left and breezed into the end zone for LSU's first score of the game. The play call caught Florida off guard, as the Gators had loaded the interior to stuff a quarterback sneak.

- **Florida 17, LSU 7: fourth-and-5 from the Florida 25-yard line, 10:14 remaining in the third quarter.** Starting quarterback Matt Flynn, in to hold a field goal attempt, executed a perfect fake and ran off-tackle for a 9-yard gain. Keiland Williams completed the scoring drive with a 4-yard touchdown three minutes later.

- **Florida 24, LSU 14: fourth-and-3 from the Florida 4-yard line, 10:22 remaining in the game.** Flynn took a shotgun snap, rolled right, moved forward as if to run, then pulled up to hit Demetrius Byrd for a touchdown.

- **Florida 24, LSU 21: fourth-and-1 from the LSU 49-yard line, 7:07 remaining.** Flynn handed off left to Jacob Hester, who was initially slowed before sneaking across the first-down marker at midfield.

- **Florida 24, LSU 21: fourth-and-inches from the Florida 6-yard line, 2:15 remaining.** Kicker Colt David had already missed from 43 and 37 yards out, so Miles kept his offense on the field. Perrilloux spun and handed off to Hester, who barely stretched the ball across the line to gain.

"I gamble more than you think," Miles said afterward. "We were going to make 'em. We just knew that."

All the conversions paid off with 1:09 left, when Hester powered into the end zone from 2 yards out. Louisiana State took a 28–24 lead—its first of the night—and the Tigers defense was left with one final task: stop Tebow.

All-America defensive tackle Glenn Dorsey answered the call. He helped LSU's four-man rush keep Tebow uncomfortable and burn plenty of time off the clock. But Florida's legendary quarterback managed to make Tigers fans nervous; he ripped off a 26-yard dash to the LSU 40-yard line with 12 seconds remaining.

Even when Kirston Pittman appeared to have Tebow dead to rights for a game-clinching sack, Tebow managed to flip the ball downfield. He received an intentional grounding penalty, but Florida got one final chance to win. Tebow took the snap at midfield, bought time, and launched a skyscraper to the end zone.

The ball fell incomplete. Louisiana State was still No. 1.

2007 ARKANSAS @ LSU

Perhaps if Les Miles had pronounced "Arkansas" correctly, his LSU team would have survived its regular-season finale vs. the unranked Razorbacks.

But Miles's insistence on saying "Ar-Kansas" (emphasis on the Sunflower State) apparently irked the Hogs—13-point underdogs—enough to inspire a 50–48 win over the No. 1 team in the country.

Don't believe in bulletin-board motivation? Read the Razorbacks' postgame quotes.

Offensive lineman Robert Felton: "I ain't no Ar-Kansas. I bet he knows how to say it now."

Defensive back Matterral Richardson: "If they had played Ar-Kansas, they might have won."

Running back Darren McFadden: "They weren't saying it right, so we wanted to let them know how to say it."

McFadden, a Heisman Trophy favorite, took his anger out in many different ways. He rushed for 206 yards and three touchdowns on 32 carries and completed three of six passes for 34 yards and another score (all after a trio of early fumbles). Much of his damage was done out of the "Wild Hog" formation, in which he lined up as a shotgun quarterback and punished the spread-out LSU defense.

The Tigers found themselves behind, 28–21, with time running out, but that didn't faze many in Baton Rouge. Louisiana State had already scored come-from-behind wins over Florida, Auburn, and Alabama, and Arkansas figured to be the next victim.

On one particularly fateful play, a Matt Flynn pass appeared to miss its primary receiver before somehow landing in the hands of tight end Richard Dickson for a 36-yard gain to the Razorbacks' 7-yard line.

Arkansas running back Darren McFadden leaps over the LSU defense during a triple-overtime win in 2007. McFadden was one of several Razorbacks players upset by Tigers coach Les Miles's mispronunciation of "Arkansas" in the lead-up to the game. AP PHOTO/ALEX BRANDON

Moments later, Flynn found Demetrius Byrd for the tying touchdown with 57 seconds left.

"You saw how the season has gone," star defensive tackle Glenn Dorsey said afterward. "We always find a way to pull it out. And I just kept waiting."

Louisiana State appeared to have its winning moment after Flynn rumbled in from 13 yards away in the first overtime period. The Tigers defense forced the Hogs into a fourth-and-10 from the 25-yard line as Death Valley sensed victory. But quarterback Casey Dick escaped the pocket and found running back Peyton Hillis wide open for a first down. On the same drive, Dick tossed a pinpoint touchdown pass to Hillis on third-and-8, and the score was again knotted.

In the second extra period, McFadden piggybacked off an explosive Felix Jones run to score from 8 yards out. That was soon followed by a tying touchdown plunge courtesy of LSU running back Jacob Hester.

Visions of six- and seven-overtime games danced in the heads of Arkansas fans; the Hogs had gone at least that far in three separate contests from 2001 to 2003. Turns out, three would suffice for Houston Nutt's team this time around.

After Hillis scored from 3 yards out and Jones' 2-point conversion rush was successful, LSU needed 8 points to stay alive. Six of them came on a Flynn pass to Brandon LaFell. The other 2? They never arrived. Flynn's final pass—fired through the teeth of a perfectly timed blitz—was intercepted by Richardson in the back of the end zone.

Arkansas had its first win over the country's No. 1 team since 1981. Louisiana State, by almost all accounts, was out of the national title race after letting its 19-game home winning streak slip away.

"Right now, a goal's off the wall," Miles said. "Zap."

The Tigers had allowed 513 total yards, including 385 on the ground, the most rushing yards surrendered in 14 years. As Miles fought off rumors that he would leave for Michigan—his alma mater and former employer—he faced the daunting task of resurrecting hope for a program that now thought its season was effectively over.

He also learned an important lesson in diction.

Wrote the *Monroe News-Star*'s Glenn Guilbeau: "The college football team formerly known as No. 1 learned the correct pronunciation of Arkansas has nothing to do with Kansas, which has a much better chance of playing in the national championship game than LSU."

2008 ALABAMA @ LSU ("THE SABAN BOWL")

A half decade turned one of the greatest sports figures in LSU history into its most hated. In 2003 Nick Saban coached the Tigers to a national title—the school's first in nearly five decades—and reestablished Louisiana State as a football power. By 2008 he was public enemy No. 1 for a fanbase that watched him leave for the NFL and return in the worst possible fashion.

Louisiana State and Alabama played a 41–34 thriller in 2007, Saban's first season with the Crimson Tide. The Tigers won and marched to their first national championship with new coach Les Miles.

In '08 the stakes were flipped. Alabama was undefeated and ranked No. 1, while LSU was set to play the spoiler on its home turf. Saban's return to Death Valley was about as cordial as one would expect; fans greeted him with a loud chorus of boos and plenty of handwritten signs (e.g., "Saban for sale. Call 1-800-sellout.") one day after lighting fire to him in effigy and chanting "Burn, Saban, burn!"

With 93,039 in attendance, it was at that point the largest crowd in the history of Tiger Stadium.

CBS announcer Verne Lundquist capped a dramatic, Bayou-themed intro package by summarizing LSU's disdain for its former hero.

"There's a psychological theory that anger is fueled by fear," Lundquist said. "If that is true, LSU fanatic fans have had their worst fears realized. Nick Saban is back as the coach of a dreaded rival."

Saban's calm demeanor throughout the week belied the intense pressure he felt. In the moments before kickoff, he screamed at his players in the locker room.

"You go out there and dominate the guy you're playing against!" he yelled, wild-eyed, his neatly combed hair flopping about. "And make his ass quit! That's our trademark! That's our M.O. as a team! That's what people know us as!"

LSU-turned-Alabama coach Nick Saban stands with quarterback John Parker Wilson before a heavily hyped 2008 game at Tiger Stadium. Wilson would later score the winning touchdown on a quarterback sneak. AP PHOTO/TONY GUTIERREZ

LEGEND

NICK SABAN

Nick Saban never wanted to coach. The kid from small-town West Virginia played safety at Kent State and drove a "big-ass" Coca-Cola truck during the off-season, figuring he would leave football behind at graduation.

That changed when Kent State's Don James asked him to stay on as a graduate assistant.

"My wife had another year of school," Saban said decades later. "So I decided to do it, even though I didn't want to go to graduate school."

His upward mobility was swift, but championships didn't exactly come pouring in when Saban reached the top of the profession in 1990. One season at Toledo, four with the Cleveland Browns (defensive coordinator under Bill Belichick), and five more with Michigan State yielded nothing legendary.

Saban rode a strong '99 season with the Spartans to an offer from LSU. And once he began applying his attention-to-detail approach—known simply as "the Process"—to southern recruits, the wins piled up. In his second season, LSU upset No. 2 Tennessee in the 2001 SEC championship game and beat Illinois in the Sugar Bowl. Two years later, the Tigers won another SEC title and took home their first national championship since 1958.

Saban was a star, and the NFL came calling; he left Baton Rouge for Miami in December 2004.

At LSU his departure was seen as angering but eventually forgivable. What he did two years later moved the needle to "traitorous." Following a pair of uninspiring seasons with the Dolphins, Saban received a massive offer from Alabama to return to the college ranks. He and his wife, Terry, decided he belonged back in the SEC.

The fallout was brutal; LSU fans slashed the car tires of one of Saban's office assistants. Message boards overflowed with threats. When Saban returned to Baton Rouge for the first time with the Crimson Tide—a 2008 win—Tigers fans incinerated him in effigy.

From a story by *ESPN the Magazine*'s Wright Thompson that year: "LSU fans hate Saban more than store-bought jambalaya, more than FEMA, more than Yankees who confuse Creole with Cajun. The man loved 'em and left 'em. This is personal. This is cultural. This hatred is . . . intergalactic. 'You could draw the analogy to Star Wars,' says Indiana professor Ed Hirt, an expert in fan behavior and why sports turn ordinary grown-ups into psychopaths. 'It is going to the dark side.'"

As Saban collected national titles at Alabama, he began to face resentment from the rest of the conference, too.

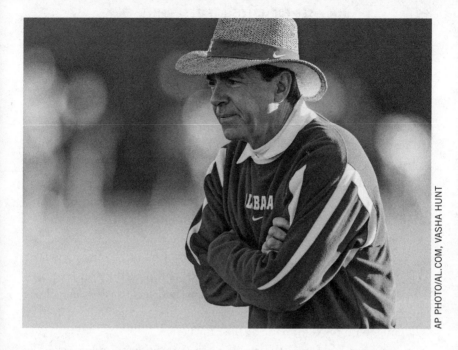

Vanderbilt coach James Franklin referred to him as "Nicky Satan" at an event in early 2013. Four months later, ex-Alabama assistant Tim Davis called Saban "the devil himself." Analysts blamed his success for the firings of highly successful coaches such as Georgia's Mark Richt and LSU's Les Miles.

Much like his former boss Belichick, Saban became so dominant that many desired to see him fail.

When the Crimson Tide lost to Ole Miss early in the 2015 season, most of the country marked it as the end of a dynasty, the end of Saban's meticulous "Process" that had yielded so many wins. But what seemed like on-point analysis turned out to be wishful thinking; Saban coached the Tide to 12 consecutive wins and its fourth title since he arrived in Tuscaloosa (he's since added a fifth).

He's the only college coach—current or former, local or national—that has lived up to the towering legacy of Paul "Bear" Bryant. And, as SEC fans are painfully aware, there's no clear end in sight to his tyranny.

"I've been a part of a team since I was nine years old," he said in 2017. "It scares me to death to figure what it's going to be like when I'm not a part of a team . . . If I felt like I couldn't do it to the standard that I want to do it, then I think that would be time not to do it.

"But I certainly don't feel like that's any time soon."

A shift in SEC West power was afoot. Louisiana State had won five straight against Alabama, but Saban brought a supremely talented team to Baton Rouge. Entering the game, the Crimson Tide had trailed for only 1 minute, 15 seconds through their first nine contests.

That dominance appeared to continue early, as quarterback John Parker Wilson led the Tide down the field. He escaped the Tigers rush, rolled to his right, and lofted a touch pass to tight end Earl Alexander, who wiggled free of his attempted tackler and stumbled toward the end zone. Just before Alexander stretched the ball across the goal line, an LSU defender knocked it out of his hand. Touchback.

Alabama didn't blink. Rashad Johnson intercepted an ill-advised Jarrett Lee pass and brought it back to the LSU 9-yard line. A few plays later, Wilson sneaked in for a 1-yard touchdown and picked up an unsportsmanlike penalty for taunting (Tigers fans had leaked Wilson's phone number on team message boards earlier that week, so Wilson mimed "Call me!" with his right hand against his helmet).

Game on: LSU used the excellent field position to move into Alabama territory, and Lee redeemed himself with a 30-yard touchdown toss to Demetrius Byrd. Alabama's Xavier Arenas fumbled away the ensuing kickoff, and LSU scored its second touchdown in 24 seconds with a 30-yard scamper by Charles Scott.

The score remained 14–7 until late in the second quarter, when Lee lost favor with the Tigers faithful again; he overthrew a deep crossing route right into the arms of Johnson, who used a wall of blockers to run the interception back 54 yards and tie the contest.

A 3-yard Glen Coffee touchdown in the third quarter and a 1-yard rebuttal by Scott in the fourth created a 21–21 tie.

Alabama went for the kill. Wilson and Coffee helped the Tide reach the Tigers' 12-yard line with one second remaining. Kicker Leigh Tiffin—perhaps the best Alabama kicker Saban ever coached—needed to hit a 29-yard field goal to win.

The kick was low, and it struck the paw of LSU linebacker Darry Beckwith. No good.

On the sideline, an exasperated Saban pulled Tiffin aside and pointed skyward, as if to say, "Kick it higher!"

None of it mattered. The most important connection of the day—LSU's Lee to Alabama's Johnson—struck again on the first play of overtime, as the Tigers passer threw into double coverage and the Tide ballhawk snared the football in the back of the end zone.

Wilson hit Julio Jones for a 23-yard gain on the ensuing possession, and then slammed home the winning score on another quarterback sneak.

As players and coaches wandered off the field, it appeared as if Saban's signals were crossed. The Alabama boss was headed toward his old locker room in what seemed like a momentary mental lapse. Instead of running into the tunnel, though, Saban sought out some of his old players and wished them well.

"We have special memories of this place," Saban told reporters afterward. "We always will. No one can ever tarnish that, no matter what they do."

Then, it was time to move on. Alabama was now 10–0 and had clinched the SEC West title. Louisiana State was once again in the shadow of its neighbor to the northeast.

2011 ALABAMA @ LSU ("THE GAME OF THE CENTURY")

When LSU visited Alabama on November 5, 2011, it was the first regular-season matchup between the country's top-two ranked teams in SEC history. Eighteen million people tuned in, the most for any regular-season game in 22 years. More than 600 media credentials were handed out, dwarfing Alabama's average of 350. Forty-five of the athletes who competed would eventually become NFL draft selections. A standing-room crowd of 101,821—including two-time NBA MVP LeBron James and former U.S. Secretary of State Condoleezza Rice—packed Bryant-Denny Stadium, while thousands more arrived in Tuscaloosa just to say they were there.

"The Game of the Century" was upon America, and fans got a gigantic dose of . . . field goals.

Missed field goals. Made field goals. All the field goals.

"Neither bruising team Saturday could even bruise the end zone," quipped the *Los Angeles Times*. "There might as well have been a sign posted on the goal line: Keep Off The Grass."

Alabama running back Trent Richardson fights off the LSU defense during "The Game of the Century" in 2011. Richardson was one of 45 players in the game to eventually become NFL draft selections. AP PHOTO/PAUL ABELL

Alabama's Cade Foster missed a 44-yarder on the opening drive. On the Crimson Tide's next drive, he missed another from 50. At the beginning of the second quarter, it was teammate Jeremy Shelley's turn; LSU blocked his 49-yard attempt to keep the score 0–0.

Finally, with 3:53 remaining in the first half, Shelley hit from 34 yards. Louisiana State struck back with an 11-play, 74-yard drive that resulted in a 19-yard Drew Alleman field goal as the clock ran out.

But the game was not just a special teams enthusiast's dream. It was a defensive showdown.

Entering that Saturday, LSU was allowing just 11.5 points per game. Alabama was even better, giving up just 6.9 per contest. Virtually every defensive player on both sides had a potential NFL future ahead of him, with 10 defenders eventually becoming first-round picks.

One of those studs—Alabama safety Mark Barron—appeared as if he might actually provide a touchdown for the impatient home crowd in the third quarter.

He intercepted a pass from LSU quarterback Jarrett Lee and took it back to the 3-yard line, but flags were down: teammate Josh Chapman was called for a block in the back, and promptly received what he later called "the biggest ass-chewing of my life" from coach Nick Saban.

Foster drilled a 46-yarder to give Alabama the lead. Minutes later, LSU's Morris Claiborne intercepted Alabama's AJ McCarron and returned it to the 'Bama 15-yard line. But the Tigers stalled, too, and called upon Alleman to kick a 30-yarder and tie the game, 6–6, with 14:13 remaining.

Of all the future NFL players who saw the field, none would be drafted higher than Alabama running back Trent Richardson, who went No. 3 overall to the Indianapolis Colts the following spring. It's curious, then, that Alabama was hesitant to use him in a few crucial spots.

Most notable was the stretch after a second-quarter screen pass that Richardson took for 39 yards—the longest offensive play of the game—to the LSU 19-yard line. Richardson didn't touch the ball over the following three plays, and 'Bama settled for a field goal. Earlier in the quarter, Richardson had ripped off a 10-yard run to the LSU 24-yard line before not factoring into the next three plays (LSU blocked the subsequent field goal attempt).

The most important moment of the game immediately followed another big Richardson run.

Alabama's Heisman Trophy candidate broke a 24-yard gain to the LSU 28-yard line. The game was tied, 6–6, and 'Bama was in great position to move ahead with a little more than 11 minutes left.

Instead of sticking to the ground, Alabama offensive coordinator Jim McElwain got tricky. He put receiver Marquis Maze behind center in a "Wildcat" formation. Maze, a former high school quarterback, faked a jet sweep handoff to DeAndrew White, and the LSU defense bit hard.

Alabama tight end Michael Williams snuck behind coverage and raced toward the end zone. Maze, pressured by the interior rush, lofted a high spiral that allowed LSU safety Eric Reid to leave his own receiver and catch up with Williams. A more accurate pass would have resulted in an easy touchdown, but 'Bama appeared to at least have a long completion as Williams leapt and secured the football in the air.

As Williams began his descent, Reid also got his hands on the ball, and the Tigers star ripped it away as both players crashed to the turf.

CBS broadcaster Verne Lundquist called it a reception, but the referees wasted little time signaling an interception at the 1-yard line. (A shocked Lundquist shouted, "Oh, no!")

"I knew they were going for the touchdown," Reid said. "So I just went deep, and, thank God, I got the ball."

Louisiana State required one more spectacular play to survive regulation. The Tigers offense sputtered after Reid's interception, and LSU was forced to punt from its own end zone. All-America punter Brad Wing—a native Australian—was excellent all game, and he nailed his most important moment.

A blistering Alabama rush forced Wing to punt the ball 0.8 seconds after receiving the snap. His booming kick sailed over Maze's head, took a big bounce, and came to a halt 73 yards from the original line of scrimmage. Alabama was suddenly back at its own 19-yard line, and neither team threatened to score over the final nine minutes.

Both defenses were so dominant that Alabama—which had two time-outs with 52 seconds remaining—didn't even attempt a game-winning drive from its own 20. On the other sideline, LSU coach Les Miles kept all three time-outs in his own pocket rather than try to force a punt.

Overtime was more of the same. McCarron was 0-for-2 on the opening drive. An illegal substitution penalty and a sack dumped the Crimson Tide back 10 yards. On came Foster to try and keep his team afloat.

"Everyone was telling me that it might come down to a field goal, and I let that get to me," the kicker later said. "I over-trained that week. I must have kicked 200 to 300 balls instead of my normal 50. So by the time the game started, my legs were almost dead."

His 52-yard attempt was ugly. It was well short and too far left.

The Tigers pounced. Quarterback Jordan Jefferson perfectly executed an option pitch on second-and-7, and running back Michael Ford raced into the end zone for what he thought was the game-winning touchdown. Officials ruled Ford out at the 7-yard line, but it didn't matter. Alleman nailed a 25-yard field goal to win it, then "shushed" the crowd by running around with his index finger over his mouth.

LSU 9, Alabama 6. "The Game of the Century" was over.

Reactions were mixed. Much like the *Los Angeles Times* had lamented the lack of touchdowns, *Detroit News* columnist Bob Wojnarski summed up many non-southerners' feelings with a Twitter joke: "Don't forget to turn your clocks back tonight to mark Bama and LSU turning football offense back half a century."

In the South, the general consensus was that history had just been made.

"The atmosphere was national championship-esque, and the game came down to the final kick," wrote the *Monroe News-Star's* Roy Lang. "What else can you ask for?"

On Sunday morning, the *Montgomery Advertiser's* front page featured a single-word headline: "Rematch?"

Alabama fell only one spot in the Bowl Championship Series rankings—to No. 3—and still had a reasonable chance at a national title game appearance. To get there, the Crimson Tide likely needed five schools to lose another game: Oklahoma State, Stanford, Boise State, Oregon, and Oklahoma.

Sure enough, all five lost before December. The most stunning development came on November 18, when 27-point underdog Iowa State beat Oklahoma State in double-overtime on the same day the Cowboys learned that four people—including women's basketball coach Kurt Budke—had died in an airplane crash.

The November chaos led to outrage everywhere but the SEC. Louisiana State was still No. 1, and Alabama was—once again—No. 2. Nick Saban's team didn't win its division, but it had a chance at a national championship.

The *Advertiser* headline proved prophetic, as did the words of Alabama offensive lineman Williams Vlachos after the Crimson Tide's regular-season loss to the Tigers.

"If we continue to keep the foot on the pedal and get better," Vlachos said, "I think we have a chance to do something very, very special this season."

2012 TEXAS A&M @ ALABAMA

There was not a serious Heisman Trophy case for Johnny Manziel. The redshirt freshman quarterback was enjoying a strong first season at Texas A&M, but anyone could poke holes in his résumé. "Johnny Football" had been elite against bad teams—Auburn, Louisiana Tech, Arkansas, SMU—while coming up way short against two ranked opponents (most recently in a loss to No. 6 LSU, when Manziel failed to pass or run for a touchdown in 73 combined attempts while throwing three interceptions).

The mid-November Heisman race was not exactly red-hot: Kansas State quarterback Collin Klein, Oregon running back Kenjon Barner, Alabama quarterback AJ McCarron, Ohio State quarterback Braxton Miller, and Notre Dame linebacker Manti Te'o were all in the mix. For the most part, the group was devoid of excitement. But all of them still had better odds than Manziel.

In one play, that changed.

The moment that beget Manziel Fever and birthed one of the most polarizing figures in college football history came with No. 15-ranked Texas A&M leading No. 1-ranked Alabama, 7–0, in the first quarter.

Facing 3rd-and-goal from the 10-yard line, Manziel took a shotgun snap. He began his progression, broke to his right as if to scramble, and smashed into the back of his offensive tackle. Bouncing away, Manziel lost control of the football and it popped into the air at eye level.

"Got him," CBS commentator Verne Lundquist said.

Then . . .

"Oh, no, they didn't!"

Manziel recaptured the football, sprinted left, and then threw across his body to receiver Ryan Swope for a wide-open touchdown.

"Oh my gracious!" Lundquist yelled, as if his delicate sensibilities had been trampled underfoot. "How about that?"

ESPN plastered the play all over its weekend coverage, and it helped Manziel's Heisman campaign spread like wildfire. He became an American hero for doing what so many others could not: knock Alabama from its perch.

Manziel's athleticism was on display from the beginning. On A&M's first drive, he shot up the middle of the field, juked past two defenders,

Texas A&M quarterback Johnny Manziel participates in a patented Aggies "yell" after upsetting Alabama in 2012. Manziel accounted for 345 total yards to launch himself into the Heisman Trophy conversation. AP PHOTO/DAVE MARTIN

and stiff-armed cornerback Deion Belue to the turf for a 29-yard gain. Running back Christine Michael capped the series with a 1-yard touchdown run to make it 7–0.

The next scoring drive resulted in Manziel's magical moment and a 14–0 advantage. Following another stop, Manziel ripped off a dazzling 32-yard run and Texas A&M soon found itself ahead, 20–0, with the first quarter still in progress. The Aggies—a first-year SEC team making its first-ever trip to Tuscaloosa—were living the pipe dream.

Unsurprisingly, the momentum did not last long. Despite a few more Houdini-esque conversions by Manziel, 'Bama rebounded to make it 20–14 at halftime.

Field goals from both sides made it 23–17 for much of the second half. Manziel produced several more big plays to prove the first two quarters were no fluke. He twice threaded perfect passes to Swope downfield— one for 28 yards, the other for 42—before tossing a beautiful 24-yard touchdown to Malcome Kennedy for a 29–17 lead with 8:37 remaining.

After a botched kickoff return, Alabama had the ball at its own 6-yard line, needing two touchdowns to win the game.

At the 6:44 mark, McCarron threw an ugly pass into the hands of Texas A&M defensive back Deshazor Everett near the sideline. The Aggies went wild, while 'Bama receiver Amari Cooper slumped his shoulders and walked away, assuming the game was over.

But the sideline judge ran into the picture and signaled that the pass was incomplete. He was right; replays showed Everett's heel had landed out of bounds. Given new life, McCarron hit Cooper for a 54-yard touchdown. Texas A&M's lead was now 29–24. Minutes later, Manziel took a sack on third-and-5, and the Aggies punted back to the Tide.

Thus began the momentary nightmare for everyone rooting against Nick Saban's team. McCarron hit Kenny Bell for 54 yards on the first play, putting the football at Texas A&M's 6-yard line. Two plays later, he did a fairly convincing Manziel impression that nearly culminated in his own Heisman moment. McCarron evaded the Aggies rush for several seconds, running to the right hash mark before circling all the way back across the field. He avoided two diving Aggies as he crossed the line of scrimmage and appeared to have a free lane to the end zone.

Just as the exhausted quarterback was about to stumble across the goal line, he was met with a violent hit by Texas A&M defensive back Dustin Harris at the 2-yard line.

Instead of a game-winning touchdown, it was fourth-and-goal.

Working out of the shotgun, McCarron rolled right and threw toward the right pylon. A&M's Everett read the play perfectly and leapt in front of Bell—the intended receiver—for a game-clinching interception.

The play capped a dramatic fourth quarter and ensured that Texas A&M's star quarterback would be revered from coast to coast.

Manziel's first-quarter scramble-and-throw became so ubiquitous that it might as well have taken place in the fourth quarter with the game on the line. The play symbolized Alabama's (very temporary) demise and saved a dreary Heisman race. His final stat line: 24-of-31 for 253 yards and two touchdowns, plus another 92 yards on the ground.

"Manziel had the kind of game people will talk about years from now," wrote Heisman expert Frank Schwab. "He was a redshirt freshman playing the No. 1 team on the road, and instead of looking nervous, he dominated . . . Many Heisman Trophy winners have their one 'Heisman moment.' On Saturday, Manziel had three and a half hours' worth of them."

2018 ROSE BOWL: GEORGIA VS. OKLAHOMA

Ask a college football fan about Baker Mayfield, and—depending on where the fan is from—you're going to get a particular section of Mayfield's Wikipedia page repeated back to you.

If the fan is from Norman, they will tell you Mayfield is one of the greatest college quarterbacks to ever play. He was a Heisman Trophy finalist in two consecutive seasons before winning the award. He posted the highest passer-efficiency rating in the history of the sport. And he won nine of every ten games he played, including three straight wins against hated Oklahoma State to help secure a trio of Big 12 titles.

If the fan is from, say, Austin, Columbus, or Lawrence, they'll bring up some other things first.

"Baker Mayfield got arrested for public intoxication."

"Baker Mayfield, delinquent scum, planted a flag at midfield of Ohio Stadium."

"Baker Mayfield grabbed his own crotch and shouted obscenities at the opposing team while Oklahoma was winning by several touchdowns."

If you talk to someone from Athens, Georgia, they'll point out an even bigger sin.

Only 13 minutes into the Rose Bowl, Mayfield made a throat-slash gesture toward the Georgia sideline and said, "It's over." Naturally, this was caught on camera live by ESPN, effectively ending any future political dreams Mayfield might have had in the Peach State.

The national semifinal game was not, in fact, over. Georgia's first Rose Bowl appearance since World War II would feature a trio of second-half lead changes and enough shifted momentum to warrant a Hollywood script.

There would also be retribution. With Oklahoma nursing a 31–24 lead in the third quarter, Mayfield took a nasty hit to his ribcage from 300-pound defensive lineman Julian Rochester, who flew in late (legally, per the officiating crew) and drove his knee into Mayfield's side.

Georgia linebacker Lorenzo Carter (7) leaps to block an Oklahoma field goal attempt during the 2018 Rose Bowl. It was one of several dramatic twists during a 54-48 Bulldogs victory that sent Georgia to the national championship game. AP PHOTO/GREGORY BULL

Suddenly, the wounded Heisman winner was a nonfactor. He took a pair of sacks as the drive died. The next time-out, he threw an interception that Bulldogs safety Dominick Sanders took back to the Sooners' 4-yard line. Georgia quickly had a 38–31 lead, and Mayfield was helpless on the next drive, too, completing two passes for a grand total of minus-2 yards.

Outside of one more brilliant scoring drive to tie the game 38–38, he was done.

Mayfield attempted just seven more passes for a total of 21 yards during Oklahoma's final four drives of the game, which netted a total of 3 points.

Without Georgia's offensive explosion, the game still would not have been close. Moments after Mayfield caught a trick-play touchdown pass for a 31–14 Sooners lead near the end of the first half, Bulldogs kicker Rodrigo Blankenship provided a much-needed spark with a 55-yard field goal.

Running back Nick Chubb ran for a 50-yard score on Georgia's first play of the third quarter, and fellow 1,000-yard rusher Sony Michel later scored from 38 yards out to tie the game, 31–31.

The 'Dawgs capitalized on Mayfield's interception with a 4-yard scoring pass from Jake Fromm to Javon Wims, and then—after watching Oklahoma put up 14 straight points, 7 of them off an uncharacteristic fumble by Michel—went on a seven-play, 59-yard drive that tied the game, 45–45, with less than a minute remaining.

Fromm, a true freshman, was instrumental down the stretch. He finished the game 20-of-29 for 210 yards, two touchdowns, and no interceptions.

Overtime yielded a pair of field goals before Georgia linebacker Lorenzo Carter made the play of the evening. On a 27-yard attempt in double overtime, Carter busted through the left side of the line, reached his hand high, and deflected Austin Seibert's kick. Two plays later, Michel—the goat-turned-hero—raced in for the game-clinching 27-yard touchdown and burst into tears as his teammates swarmed him.

Mayfield's storied career was over, and the 'Dawgs were headed to the national championship game.

Both teams wandered around the field in the immediate aftermath, and Georgia linebacker Davin Bellamy felt Mayfield needed some advice. Cameras caught Bellamy shouting a now-trademarked phrase at the Heisman winner as he stepped off the college gridiron for the final time in his career: "Humble yourself!"

PART 5: ATLANTA, HERE WE COME

On February 23, 1994, the SEC announced it would be moving its championship game from Birmingham—which had just completed the second year of a five-year contract—to Atlanta. The coup shocked fans and lawmakers alike.

"I cannot help but feel we have not been dealt with fairly in this matter," Birmingham mayor Richard Arrington said.

The *Birmingham News* was a little more direct. "SEC knifed Magic City in the back," read the headline of one column.

When the news broke, SEC commissioner Roy Kramer was on vacation in Norway, and the league office refused to comment until he returned. Representatives from the Georgia Dome, Atlanta Sports Council, and Atlanta Chamber of Commerce also declined to speak with reporters in the immediate aftermath.

In a private phone call with Arrington after the decision was made public, Kramer gave two reasons for the move: the University of Alabama's unfair home-field advantage (at the time, the Crimson Tide played half of its home games at Legion Field) and the weather-proof environment at the state-of-the-art Georgia Dome.

"Big-city appeal" and TV ratings were also clear factors, wrote *Montgomery Advertiser* sports editor Jim Johnston. He agreed that the move made sense, but it still left a bad taste in his mouth.

Former SEC commissioner Roy Kramer executes the pre-game coin flip before the 2015 SEC Championship Game. Kramer was responsible for creating the first-ever conference championship game in 1992. TODD J. VAN EMST/SEC VIA AP

"The reasons for the change aren't troubling," Johnston wrote. "The problem lies in the way it's been handled."

Seeing as league offices were—and still are—headquartered in Birmingham, the SEC could not simply look past the city's outrage. Kramer later reported that several friends and colleagues refused to speak to him. But he and the school presidents had decided a conference championship game in Atlanta was too good of an opportunity to pass up. One of the South's largest cities was at the forefront of the international athletics scene, with the Georgia Dome serving as a primary piece of Atlanta's successful bid for the 1996 Olympics.

When the game finally kicked off in December, Alabama was still upset about the circumstances. The final score didn't help things.

1994 SEC CHAMPIONSHIP GAME: FLORIDA VS. ALABAMA

The venue was different, but the names on the scoreboard remained the same.

No. 3-ranked Alabama arrived at the Georgia Dome with an 11–0 record, in pursuit of its second national title in three seasons. No. 6 Florida, which had upset Alabama in the freezing rain at Legion Field the previous December, was hoping to claim a second consecutive SEC title. The Gators' mental resolve—or lack thereof—was a serious concern, as Steve Spurrier's team had just suffered through the infamous "Choke at Doak" vs. Florida State the week before.

A Georgia Dome–record 74,751 fans were on hand, and Alabama made the new digs feel like home early.

On the Tide's first drive, Heisman finalist Jay Barker fired a third-and-4 bullet across his body to the middle of the field. Two Florida defenders collided as 'Bama receiver Curtis Brown hauled in the pass at midfield and ran in for a 70-yard touchdown.

Florida's "Fun 'n' Gun" offense had some firepower of its own. Sophomore quarterback Danny Wuerffel had thrown for 14 touchdowns since taking over for Terry Dean in mid-October, and fans caught a glimpse of the future as Wuerffel found freshman receiver Reidel Anthony several times early.

The pair connected for a few first downs before Wuerffel tossed a perfect 26-yard scoring pass to Anthony that knotted the game, 7–7.

The teams traded field goals, traded interceptions, and traded punts before the scoreboard changed again. Gators linebacker Sam McCorkle blocked a punt that gave Florida excellent field position, and star running back Fred Taylor capitalized. He picked up three first downs on the ensuing drive—two through the air, one on the ground—before Wuerffel sneaked into the end zone for a 17–10 halftime lead.

In the fourth, Florida fans got a nightmare flashback of the 1992 title game, in which Alabama's Antonio Langham intercepted a Shane Matthews pass and returned it for the game-winning touchdown.

This time, it was Wuerffel who tossed a second-and-10 pass toward the right sideline, where it was bobbled and then intercepted by freshman linebacker Dwayne Rudd. The Crimson Tide defender took it to the

LEGEND
DANNY WUERFFEL

As Danny Wuerffel tore through the SEC in 1996 en route to All-America honors, a Heisman Trophy, and a national championship, *Sports Illustrated* ran a feature story on his impossibly clean image.

Among the anecdotes: Wuerffel was selected as Playboy's Scholar Athlete of the Year, but he turned down the "honor" for moral reasons. As far as anybody knew, he had never lost his temper or used a cuss word. When local reporters found a small character blemish—fingernail-chewing—Wuerffel broke the habit and showed off "perfectly manicured" nails not long after.

Florida football had nothing to worry about off the field, and it sure as sin didn't have anything to worry about on it. Wuerffel put together two of the greatest passing seasons in NCAA history in '95 and '96, helping Steve Spurrier's "Fun 'n' Gun" offense ascend from oddity to legend.

His Gators career effectively began in 1993, when—after throwing three interceptions and asking Spurrier to put him back in the game—he drove the offense across midfield and tossed a 28-yard touchdown pass to walk-on receiver Chris Doering that beat Kentucky with three seconds remaining.

Two years earlier, Spurrier had recruited the quarterback out of Fort Walton Beach, Florida, where he was not only Florida's best high school football player, but valedictorian at the city's public school. The Wuerffel family was a military family of sorts; Danny's father, Jon, was an Air Force chaplain, and his various assignments landed his family in places such as South Carolina, Colorado, and Spain.

Danny, the second of two kids, had a weird throwing motion that looked a bit like he was throwing a shotput. It didn't deter him from record-setting prep and college careers.

His pro football career was much less prolific. Wuerffel spent six NFL seasons with New Orleans, Green Bay, Chicago, and Washington, and—amid that run—managed to win the 2000 World Bowl with the Rhein Fire in NFL Europe.

Following a short reunion with Spurrier during the Redskins' 2002 season, Wuerffel retired and began a new career with nonprofit Desire Street Ministries. Hurricane Katrina wiped out his home in 2005, and he was diagnosed with a dangerous immune system disorder in 2011, but he has always kept his work with his organization at the forefront.

Now the face of Desire Street, Wuerffel was featured in the 2015 ESPN documentary *Wuerffel's Way*. He still keeps close tabs on the Gators, and his statue stands next to Spurrier's and Tim Tebow's outside Ben Hill Griffin Stadium.

From the game-winning throw at Kentucky to the national championship game, No. 7 was not only one of Florida's best players, but one of the best to throw the football for any school.

"It's kind of like bookends, my first and my last were really special games," he said in 2015. "Sometimes I wake up and wonder if my life was an amazing dream or some movie."

Florida's Steve Spurrier and Alabama's Gene Stallings share a moment after
Florida's win in the 1994 SEC Championship Game. The rivals put on a show at
the Georgia Dome, which was hosting the SEC title game for the first time.
AP PHOTO/DAVE MARTIN

house, and the Gators, who had not scored since the second quarter, were
suddenly on the wrong end of a 23–17 deficit with time slipping away.

Coming off the "Choke at Doak"—a 28-point meltdown at rival
Florida State that ended in a tie—Spurrier's team needed to show some
serious resolve. And it did, thanks to a play called "Hobble Off."

By design, Wuerffel feigned an injury after a hard hit and limped off
the field. On came backup Eric Kresser, a strong-armed sophomore who
had seen limited action. Alabama, assuming Florida would play conser-
vatively after Wuerffel's "injury," let its guard down, and Kresser lofted a
25-yard completion to Ike Hilliard.

Spurrier then grabbed Wuerffel and sent him back onto the field.

The Head Ball Coach kept open his bag of tricks. After Taylor converted a fourth-and-1 run from the 33, Wuerffel threw a long backwards
lateral to Anthony, who put his head down and picked up a few yards.
Moments later, the Gators ran the same play to Chris Doering, who

caught the ball and pulled up to throw instead of run. He hit receiver Aubrey Hill along the left sideline for a 20-yard completion to the 2.

On first down, Wuerffel was supposed to sneak into the end zone, but he called an audible when he saw Alabama packing the line of scrimmage. Instead of running, he dropped back and found Doering on a slant in the back of the end zone. Florida had a 24–23 lead it would not relinquish.

A final interception from Barker on fourth-and-13 sealed the game with 54 seconds remaining. Afterward, reporters grilled Alabama coach Gene Stallings about his decision to kick an extra point instead of go for a 2-point conversion, which would have led to overtime.

Stallings's explanation: the Crimson Tide would not have wanted to be stuck with a 5-point lead and have the Gators win with two field goals.

Spurrier's response: "Have we ever kicked two field goals in a game?"

1997 SEC CHAMPIONSHIP GAME: TENNESSEE VS. AUBURN

For the first time since the SEC championship game's inception, Steve Spurrier and the Florida Gators were not champions of the East. That honor fell to a rival the Gators had defeated back in September: Tennessee.

Star quarterback Peyton Manning and the Vols had lost at the Swamp, but won every other game while Florida suffered a pair of upset losses. It was a scenario borne "as much by the failures of others as the Vols' own performance," per *Nashville Tennessean* columnist David Climer.

Somehow, Manning—0–4 against Florida in his career—had No. 3-ranked Tennessee in position to potentially win a national championship. The Vols' only remaining roadblock was No. 11-ranked Auburn, but national prognosticators seemed more worried about Manning's Heisman odds than they did about UT's fate in Atlanta.

The All-American put up big numbers early. He hit running back Jamal Lewis on a boundary screen for 25 yards on the opening play, and capped the drive with a 40-yard touchdown pass to Peerless Price.

Auburn had a star quarterback of its own. Fifth-year senior Dameyune Craig responded to Manning's opening statement with 69-yard pass to Hicks Poor on the ensuing drive. The Tigers kicked a field goal and began a dominant stretch of defensive play.

Tennessee quarterback Peyton Manning fakes a handoff against Auburn in the 1997 SEC Championship Game. The Volunteers win was a long time coming; as Auburn coach Terry Bowden noted, "They've been the bridesmaid an awful lot." AP PHOTO/RIC FELD

"For a half, at least," wrote J. C. Clemons of the *Montgomery Advertiser*, "[Manning] wasn't even the most outstanding quarterback on the field, let alone player."

Auburn forced a fumble by Vols wideout Marcus Nash and returned it for a 10–7 lead. A few more stops helped Craig and the Tigers O extend it to 20–7.

The Vols eventually responded with a 5-yard touchdown from Manning to Jeremaine Copeland with 11:58 remaining in the third quarter. Later in the third, Tennessee moved into position to take the lead, but a Manning pass bounced off Copeland's hands and into the arms of Auburn defensive back Jayson Bray, who returned it 77 yards to set up a touchdown pass from Craig to fullback Fred Beasley.

With a little more than 20 minutes to play, Auburn had a 27–17 lead. Tennessee had turned the ball over five times, had dropped a handful of passes, and would later surrender another fumble as well as a blocked extra-point return.

But as it turned out, the Vols could play some defense, too. Manning led two touchdown drives—including a 46-yard touchdown toss to Price and a 73-yard screen pass to Nash—that gave Tennessee a 30–29 lead, which the UT defense was forced to preserve over the final 11-plus minutes.

Defensive end Leonard Little made a pair of crucial sacks, including one on third-and-13 with four and a half minutes remaining, that helped Tennessee seal the win. After so many failures in big moments during the Manning era, Rocky Top had a signature win.

"Maybe it's just Tennessee's year," Auburn coach Terry Bowden said. "They've been the bridesmaid an awful lot. Maybe they were just due."

1998 SEC CHAMPIONSHIP GAME: TENNESSEE VS. MISSISSIPPI STATE

It couldn't happen like this, could it? Tennessee, ranked No. 1 in the country for the first time in 42 years and heavily favored over No. 23 Mississippi State in the 1998 SEC championship game, found itself down 14–10 in the fourth quarter.

MSU's Kevin Prentiss had just returned a punt 83 yards for the go-ahead touchdown. The Bulldogs celebrated with gusto. The Georgia Dome shrieked. ABC announcer Keith Jackson shouted, "Lightning has struck!"

With Peyton Manning now playing for the Indianapolis Colts, the Volunteers had a new leader at quarterback: Tee Martin. The junior from Mobile, Alabama, had guided Tennessee to wins over No. 2 Florida,

LEGEND
PEYTON MANNING

Peyton Manning's father thought he was going to choose Michigan. So did his older brother. Months of speaking with coaches, studying media guides, and networking with other high-profile prep quarterbacks led to a blue-blooded list of finalists that included Tennessee, Ole Miss, Florida . . . and Michigan.

"For a while there, I really thought he was going to go to Michigan," said older brother Cooper. "It was just kind of outside the box . . . I think he kind of liked that scene."

Wolverines quarterbacks coach Cam Cameron had spent much of 1993 persuading New Orleans's top football recruit—the son of Mississippi legend Archie Manning—that he needed to skip the SEC and fly north to the Big Ten.

The South posed a few dilemmas. Florida already had its quarterback of the future in Danny Wuerffel. Manning had reservations about Tennessee because the Vols would have to play against Ole Miss—the school where his father was a hero and his mother was homecoming queen—twice before his graduation. Then, there was the circus of overzealous fans and reporters in Oxford.

"Ole Miss is my school and it will always be my school," Archie said on the day of Peyton's commitment. "But I think the whole Mississippi thing may have gotten out of control as far as he was concerned. It may have been too much for anybody."

So Michigan made sense. And up until the day before his commitment, it remained a possibility.

The Midwest pipe dream ended when Manning took a walk on January 24, 1994, did some deep thinking, and returned home to tell his father he had made his choice: Tennessee.

On Rocky Top, he beat out fellow quarterback recruit Branndon Stewart for playing time during their freshman year, took over as full-time starter in 1995, and immediately began living up to the hype. That season, the Vols finished as the No. 2-ranked team in the country after going 11–1 with a win over No. 4 Ohio State in the Citrus Bowl. The highlight of the year was a 41–14 dismantling of No. 12 Alabama at Legion Field, in which Manning threw for 184 yards and two touchdowns—and ran in another score—in the first quarter alone.

Off the field, he was known as a meticulous student of the gridiron.

"You never wanted to tell Peyton one thing and then tell him something else later, because he'd have the notes," coach Phillip Fulmer said. "He'd say, 'Coach, let's go back and look at that.' Then I'd have to say, 'Well, okay.'"

The following year, Tennessee won 10 more games and captured another Citrus Bowl trophy against No. 11 Northwestern. With the New York Jets expected to select Manning No. 1 overall in the 1997 NFL Draft, many figured the junior would leave Tennessee early. On the morning of the big decision, the *Knoxville News-Sentinel* implied his departure with a headline that read, "Insiders expect him to go pro."

Much like his recruitment decision, Manning kept people guessing. He opened his press conference with a few statements that made it seem as if he was leaving.

Then, the verdict.

"I've made up my mind, and I don't expect to ever look back," he said. "I'm gonna stay at the University of Tennessee."

The room erupted. Tennessee was once

again a national title contender. Never mind that Manning would lose to Florida for a fourth time that September; he carried the Vols to a No. 3 ranking, an SEC championship, and a shot at winning it all vs. No. 2 Nebraska in the Orange Bowl.

Both his team goals and his individual goals fell short, as Michigan defensive back Charles Woodson won the Heisman Trophy over Manning a few weeks before Nebraska clobbered Tennessee by 25.

But the star quarterback was on to bigger things. By April he was the face of the Indianapolis Colts, and he eventually won two Super Bowl rings while rewriting the NFL record book. Following a win over Carolina in Super Bowl 50, the 39-year-old quarterback retired as the league's all-time leader in passing yards and passing touchdowns.

"Almost 19 years ago to the day, I announced my decision to forgo the draft and stay at the University of Tennessee for my senior year," he said during his retirement speech in 2015. "It was one of the smartest decisions I've ever made. I cherished my time in Knoxville, especially my senior year. And I want Vols fans everywhere to know the unique role that you've played in my life."

Tennessee players drench coach Phillip Fulmer with Gatorade following a hard-fought win in the 1998 SEC Championship Game. The Volunteers' win propelled them into the first-ever BCS title game, which they won. AP PHOTO/DAVE MARTIN

No. 7 Georgia, and No. 10 Arkansas—as well as a thrilling Week 1 win on the road against Donovan McNabb and No. 17 Syracuse—en route to a second consecutive SEC East title.

If the Vols could outlast the Bulldogs, they would be headed to the inaugural BCS national championship game with a chance to win their first national title in 31 years.

Down by 4 points with 8:33 remaining, Martin and the UT offense took the field for their rebuttal.

A pass interference penalty helped the Vols move near midfield, and then a first-down run by Travis Stephens put Tennessee at the Mississippi State 41-yard line.

On the following play, Martin—standing in against a fierce MSU rush—lofted a deep rainbow down the left sideline and Peerless Price made a spectacular catch as he crashed out of bounds near the end zone. The side judge raised his arms to signal a touchdown, and the Georgia Dome once again lost its sanity.

The Vols were not done. Corey Terry sacked Bulldogs quarterback Wayne Madkin on the next drive, forcing a fumble that Tennessee recovered. Martin capitalized with a 21-yard touchdown pass to Cedrick Wilson on the next play, and the orange suddenly had a 24–14 lead.

Tennessee was on its way to Phoenix to play for the national title.

The Vols had overcome the loss of 14 players to the NFL and a season-ending injury to star running back Jamal Lewis to weave through a difficult schedule without blemish.

"There's been something magical about this team," linebacker Raynoch Thompson said afterward. "We believe in each other, and have earned everything we've gotten. Some people say we're lucky. I say we've been good."

2001 SEC CHAMPIONSHIP GAME: LSU VS. TENNESSEE

Let's rewind to a time when Nick Saban was not a household name. In 2001, Saban's second season in the Bayou, the LSU Tigers won a weak West division to earn the school's first-ever trip to the conference title game. Saban's task in Atlanta: outcoach 10-year SEC veteran Phil Fulmer, who had already won a national title and appeared to be on his way to another one.

The Vols had climbed to No. 2 in the BCS rankings and simply needed to dispatch of LSU to punch a ticket to their second national title game in four seasons. Tennessee's roster was littered with NFL talent—John Henderson keyed a tough defensive front while Jason Witten and Donté Stallworth provided reliable receiving options— and the Vols

LSU quarterback Matt Mauck jumps into his teammates' arms during the 2001 SEC Championship Game. Entering the contest, Mauck had only played in one half all season. STEVE FRANZ/LSU

boasted a consistent passer, Casey Clausen, to go along with the SEC's leading rusher, Travis Stephens.

Following an upset win over No. 2 Florida the previous week, the Vols had returned to campus to find nearly 10,000 fans waiting for them. The Rocky Top faithful handed out roses and players clenched them with their teeth; a Rose Bowl berth seemed inevitable.

On the other side, LSU had won five straight games to crack the Top 25 and sneak into the title contest. Almost all of the stars were holdovers from the pre-Saban era, including All-America wide receiver Josh Reed, who set the SEC single-season receiving record (1,740) that year.

It was a feel-good moment for a program on the rise, not a legitimate threat; Tennessee's Fulmer had never lost to a team ranked between numbers 18 and 25 in the polls.

In fact, Tennessee had defeated LSU by 8 points earlier in the season, and held a 19–4–3 all-time series lead on the Tigers. The Vols were in the midst of a seven-game winning streak, including that thrilling 34–32 win over Florida.

It wasn't until the fourth quarter of the SEC title game that Vols fans really began to sweat.

Up 17–16 entering the final period, Tennessee allowed LSU to convert a key third down in Vols territory. Then, it allowed a hole to open for Tigers backup quarterback Matt Mauck—who, entering the championship, had played only one half the entire season—to scamper for the go-ahead touchdown.

"Tennessee is bigger and stronger on both sides of the ball," CBS analyst Todd Blackledge said before the opening kickoff. "The question for LSU: When Tennessee hits tonight, will LSU be ready to hit back, and hit back for 60 minutes?"

The Tigers answered this, emphatically.

Saban's prized position group—the defensive backs—made the game's key play, stripping Stallworth in LSU territory to preserve a 24–20 lead with 8:30 remaining. With the Tigers driving the other way, CBS showed a fan holding a sign that read "We came to mess things up."

Announcer Verne Lundquist laughed.

"I love the sign," he said. "LSU might mess things up."

Just as he spoke, Mauck unleashed a deep ball to Reed, who was ambushed by a pair of Vols defenders before the ball arrived. The penalty gave LSU a first down at the Tennessee 13-yard line, and the Tigers moved the chains again before Saban was forced to make one of the most important calls of his career.

Facing fourth-and-goal from the 1-yard line with 2:28 remaining, Saban elected to forgo a field goal (which would put LSU up 7) and instead sent second-string running back Domanick Davis over the top of the offensive line for the game's final score.

Tennessee's dream of a national title was extinguished.

"After the game I remember seeing how dejected the Tennessee fans were. They were in disbelief," Mauck said later. "It seemed a foregone conclusion that they'd win ... there's a backup QB and second-string RB and we still can't win. It was a shock for most Tennessee fans."

Fulmer led the team to an 8–5 record the following season, and recorded at least three losses in every year afterward until his departure in December 2008.

Meanwhile, LSU went on to win the 2003 national title under Saban, and then another in 2007 under Les Miles. The Tigers were a consistent national power for more than a decade after their upset win, while the Vols quickly faded from the ranks of America's elite.

2008 SEC CHAMPIONSHIP GAME: FLORIDA VS. ALABAMA

In 1989, a 25-year-old Urban Meyer showed up at Nick Saban's front door in Houston to ask for a job. Saban had just been hired for his first head coaching gig at Toledo, but was in the midst of finishing a playoff run with the NFL's Oilers.

When Meyer knocked, Saban wasn't home, but his wife, Terry, was. She sat Meyer down for an interview and came away impressed.

Despite the positive review, Saban never called Meyer back.

Meyer landed an assistant job at Colorado State, where he coached wide receivers for six seasons. In 1996 he left for the same job at Notre Dame, just 150 miles from where Saban was building a winner at Michigan State. The schools met three times—all MSU wins—before Saban left for LSU and Meyer took his first head coaching job at Bowling Green.

Now, after both had won national titles with SEC teams, they met in a battle of No. 1 vs. No. 2 at the Georgia Dome. The winner was effectively guaranteed a spot in the national championship game.

Alabama-Florida had defined the Southeastern Conference during the '90s, and the rivalry was about to be reignited. Saban's Crimson Tide

Florida quarterback Tim Tebow (left) and coach Urban Meyer (right) revel in a second national championship in three years. Tebow completed 5 of 5 pass attempts for 72 yards and a touchdown in the final quarter against Oklahoma.
AP PHOTO/DAVE MARTIN

was 12–0 and No. 1 after barely sneaking into the preseason rankings. Meyer's Gators were 11–1 and No. 2 with several holdovers—including Heisman Trophy winner Tim Tebow—from his national championship team two seasons prior.

Tebow was the focus of Florida's opening drive. The senior rushed four times for 19 yards and threw three times for 25 yards and a touchdown. When he was in the open field, he appeared to deliver hits against the Alabama defense, instead of the other way around.

Alabama countered with a major weapon of its own: wide receiver Julio Jones. He snagged a John Parker Wilson pass and raced down the field for a 64-yard gain. All-SEC running back Glen Coffee finished the drive with an impressive run, juking away from a tackler and diving across the goal line for the tying score.

LEGEND

TIM TEBOW

In the summer of 2017, hundreds of thousands of baseball fans showed up in minor-league ballparks across the South to see Tim Tebow. The 29-year-old rookie outfielder drew wild numbers during his time with the Columbia (South Carolina) Fireflies and the St. Lucie (Florida) Mets, giving marathon autograph sessions before and after games and earning thunderous cheers for every hit.

Lower-level baseball had not seen such fanatic turnout since 1994, when NBA legend Michael Jordan briefly retired from basketball and began a stint with the Birmingham Barons.

If college football has ever produced an athlete who could rival Jordan's fame, it's probably Tebow. His trademark jump passes and pulverizing runs helped Florida win national titles in 2006 and 2008, sandwiching a sophomore Heisman Trophy season in 2007. The Gators went 13–1 and won the Sugar Bowl his senior year, and then he parlayed his first-round NFL draft selection into several memorable moments with the Denver Broncos.

But people didn't attend baseball games in Lexington, Tampa, or Charleston nearly a decade after his Gators career just because of his on-field résumé. They also showed up because they connected with the message that Tebow proudly referenced on his eye black during games at Florida: "For God so loved the world that he gave his one and only Son, that whoever believes in him shall not perish but have eternal life."

The Philippines-born, Florida-raised son of missionaries was the sports world's most public link to Jesus Christ. And that connection grew stronger during his time with the Denver Broncos, when a seemingly innocuous move—going to one knee and pointing upward—made him even more of a household name. "Tebowing" became the trend of 2011, as the move was both emulated and mocked in backyards across the country.

Whether it was his immense success at Florida, his ultra-positive attitude, or his faith, Tebow always received plenty of pushback from America.

That incredulousness reared its head again when the New York Mets signed Tebow—a part-time SEC Network analyst who had not played organized baseball since high school—to a minor-league deal nearly four years after his final NFL game. As fans complained that the signing was simply a public relations move, Mets general manager Sandy Alderson insisted it was a "baseball decision."

By the end of the following season, after Tebow had made plenty of money for the organization but proved himself to be a lackluster prospect, Alderson admitted the signing had plenty to do with Tebow's "celebrity" and the "entertainment business." He even revealed a joke the team had planted in the preseason media guide: The "scout" listed as the one who signed Tebow was actually the franchise's director of merchandising.

Through it all, Tebow stayed dedicated to his craft, and to his fans. Each small town he visited buzzed with anticipation. In Rome, Georgia, during a road series, the community knew that Tebow had made a Monday morning visit to the YMCA on 2nd Avenue and eaten a Tuesday night meal with family members at Chili's on McCall Boulevard.

Many of his adorers held copies of his most recent book, *Shaken*, in hopes that he would sign it (he did). Some held out Florida Gators helmets and jerseys. A sizable number of young women charged the front row in hopes of procuring selfies.

Before the final game in Rome, a local group of adults with special needs sang the national anthem. Afterward, Tebow delayed the opening pitch while greeting them and signing their T-shirts. They presented him with a gift—a shirt signed by hundreds of local schoolchildren—as a thank-you for his charity work in the area.

"With him, success means trying your best, touching lives and enjoying the journey," wrote the *Orlando Sentinel*'s David Whitley following Tebow's final game of 2017. "On this one, Tebow might have looked like a joke at times. The really funny thing is his critics ended up looking a lot worse."

The teams traded field goals in the second quarter and touchdowns in the third. Tebow continued to make crucial plays while Alabama's rushing attack—featuring Coffee and future Heisman winner Mark Ingram—found room to work.

A 10-play, 65-yard drive gave the Crimson Tide a 20–17 lead heading into the fourth quarter. At that juncture, a CBS graphic showed that Tebow had a career 0–5 record when trailing in the second half.

He didn't let that narrative last long.

Tebow directed Florida down the field, aided by running backs Jeff Demps and Emmanuel Moody, as well as a 15-yard facemask penalty on 'Bama. As the Gators approached the red zone, Tebow hit David Nelson for 13 yards, and then tossed another first-down completion to tight end Aaron Hernandez.

Two plays later, he ran the option to his left and flipped the football to Demps for a 24–20 lead.

Florida quickly forced an Alabama punt, and Tebow cemented his SEC legacy. He threw a perfect pass to Louis Murphy for a 33-yard gain, then found Hernandez for 15 more. On third-and-goal from the 5-yard line—with Alabama attempting to keep it a one-score game—Tebow threw a slant to his roommate, Riley Cooper, to seal the conference championship with 2:50 remaining.

"This guy is unbelievable," CBS commentator Gary Danielson said of Tebow. "C'mon now. You can't do this stuff . . . He's taking on SEC linebackers and defensive ends and tackles all year, and he still makes those throws here down the stretch?

"If you're gonna vote [for the Heisman], you gotta at least pause and think, 'Should I vote for this guy and what he's done this year?'"

Tebow, winner of the award the previous season, had a vote of his own to use. Before the game, he had told reporters he would make a careful decision, naming other quarterbacks such as Texas Tech's Graham Harrell, Texas's Colt McCoy, and Oklahoma's Sam Bradford (the eventual winner).

In the moment, he was clearly not thinking of the Heisman. As Florida's special teams huddled before kicking off with an 11-point lead, Tebow ran over to his teammates, crashed into them, and screamed at them in an effort to avoid a letdown.

The Gators obliged. After successful kickoff coverage, Florida's defense hit Wilson as he threw and cornerback Joe Haden grabbed the game-ending interception.

As Saban steamed on the opposite sideline, Meyer got a Gatorade bath from his players. The Florida coach thanked his star quarterback (5-for-5 for 72 yards and a touchdown in the final frame) for the win.

"That fourth quarter was vintage Tim Tebow," Meyer said. "I don't know the entire history of the University of Florida, but I can imagine that drive and that fourth quarter will go down as one of the greatest ever."

2009 SEC CHAMPIONSHIP GAME: ALABAMA VS. FLORIDA

Alabama made Tim Tebow cry twice. The first time, he was a senior at Nease High in Ponte Vedra, Florida, trying to make his college decision.

A star quarterback with several impressive offers, Tebow included USC, Michigan, and LSU on his list of final schools. But there were only two he was seriously interested in: Florida and Alabama.

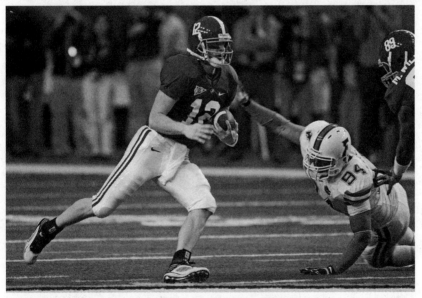

Alabama quarterback Greg McElroy escapes the pocket during a win over Florida in the 2009 SEC Championship Game. Named MVP of the game, McElroy's touchdown pass to Colin Peek gave the Crimson Tide a 26–13 lead.
AP PHOTO/ JOHN BAGEMORE

Florida QB Tim Tebow realizes defeat is nigh. Later, as he knelt on the Florida sideline, he would shed the most famous tears in SEC history. "He's a great player," Alabama wideout Julio Jones said. "But man, we're tired of him."
AP PHOTO/JOHN BAZEMORE

He was scheduled to attend a press conference to announce his choice, but he couldn't make up his mind. People told him to pray, but he said he'd been doing that "for 10 years" and still didn't have an answer. On the eve of his big moment, he called Alabama coach Mike Shula to give him the news: he would be attending the University of Florida.

Shula was gracious, so much so that Tebow began to cry.

If Florida fans knew the gravity of that decision at the time, they probably would've shed (happy) tears, too.

Four years later, the Gators senior was a Heisman Trophy winner who had helped Urban Meyer win two national titles. Florida was on a 22-game winning streak, ranked No. 1 and poised to win its second consecutive SEC title. The opponent: Alabama, which was also undefeated and held the No. 2 spot.

It was an epic rematch of the schools' 2008 SEC championship game, in which Tebow and the Gators escaped with a 31–20 win and went on to beat Oklahoma in the national title game.

In 2009 the pieces were in place for an all-time great Florida team, as Tebow and the offense were complemented by the country's No. 1 defense. Problem was, Alabama was improved, too. Saban's defense was allowing just 233 yards and 10 points per game. Future first-round picks littered the Crimson Tide D, and they wanted revenge after a close loss the previous season.

Alabama flexed its muscles out of the gate. The Tide stuffed Tebow and the Gators multiple times, and 'Bama running back Mark Ingram sliced through the middle of the line for a 9–0 lead in the first quarter.

Tebow was losing the spotlight to his Alabama counterpart, Greg McElroy. The first-year starter executed a beautiful cut block for Ingram along the sideline, and then fired a perfectly placed spiral to Marquis Maze for a 34-yard catch-and-run. On third-and-5 from the Florida 22, McElroy scrambled around several defenders and tight-roped the sideline with a hopscotch move that CBS broadcaster Verne Lundquist called "a Baryshnikov."

The Tide kicked a 34-yard field goal for a 12–3 lead.

Tebow finally responded. The senior weaved around the Alabama defense for a 23-yard gain, then danced through the defensive line for a

15-yarder. Just outside of the red zone, he pulled the ball from running back Jeff Demps's belly and fired a touchdown pass to David Nelson, cutting the deficit to 12–10.

Alabama offensive coordinator Jim McElwain dialed up the perfect counter.

Florida blitzed a cornerback, and McElroy dumped a screen to Ingram that turned into a 69-yard gain to the Florida 3-yard line. On the next play, Ingram took a handoff to the left and plowed into the end zone for a 19–10 lead.

The Crimson Tide running back entered the game with a strong chance to win the Heisman. Thus far, he had outplayed Tebow—another Heisman contender—in Atlanta and had just broken the Tide's single-season rushing record. His success was remarkable given a major off-field burden: his father, a former NFL wide receiver, was in the midst of a seven-year prison sentence for bank fraud and money laundering, and was awaiting further sentencing for failing to appear on his initial start date.

His quarterback, McElroy, was well on his way to championship game MVP honors. He hit Maze for 28 yards down the right sideline, then capped the drive with a touch pass to Colin Peek for a 26–13 advantage.

It was Ingram's turn again. Bouncing off tacklers—and drawing comparisons to Florida legend Emmitt Smith, who was in attendance and also wore No. 22 during his college career—he ripped off a pair of 10-yard gains and then a 1-yard scoring plunge on a statement drive that put the Gators in a hole they could not escape from.

Tebow led the Gators back down the field, but a potential scoring pass to Hernandez was picked off by 'Bama corner Javier Arenas.

Later, as the final seconds ticked away, Tebow knelt on the sideline and shed the most famous tears in SEC history. His pursuit of a third national title was over, as was his attempt to become the second player to win two Heisman Trophies.

Upon seeing Tebow crying on the Georgia Dome video board, Alabama fans let out a tremendous roar. On the Tide sideline, Ingram and Saban—yes, Nick Saban—leapt into the air for a shoulder bump. Soon after, Ingram and wideout Julio Jones mocked the "Gator Chomp" with exaggerated arm motions.

"He's a great player," Jones said of Tebow, "but man, we're tired of him."

The Sunday edition of the *Palm Beach Post* featured a close-up of Tebow's red eyes and some rationalization from Nelson, his receiver.

"Everything we've done, everything we worked for, and everything we wanted was for this moment," Nelson said. "For a year and a half, we've trained for this moment. And to train that hard and train that long and just not come through, it's heartbreaking."

Instead, it was Alabama's work that paid off. Ingram's big day (189 combined rushing and receiving yards, three touchdowns) was enough to earn him the Heisman Trophy, and the Tide went on to defeat Texas in the Rose Bowl for its first national title in 17 years.

Tebow and the Gators romped over Cincinnati in the Sugar Bowl, but the win couldn't quite erase the image of the star quarterback tearing up as his career—one of the most storied in college football history—came to a close.

"Tebow, more than any other Gator, earned those tears," wrote the *Post*'s Dave George. "Every salty one."

2012 SEC CHAMPIONSHIP GAME: ALABAMA VS. GEORGIA

Record-setting Georgia quarterback Aaron Murray had his team on the Alabama 8-yard line with time slipping off the clock. A touchdown would deny No. 2-ranked 'Bama a chance at its third national title in four seasons, and give No. 3-ranked Georgia a ticket to the BCS national championship game.

Murray appeared to have time for two more plays. Two chances to win. The Georgia Dome was on edge. Never before had there been such a dramatic conclusion to an SEC title game.

The next play changed the careers of numerous players and coaches.

"Like probably everybody out here, I don't think we're ever gonna get over that game," Bulldogs offensive coordinator Mike Bobo said the following spring. "The bottom line is you're never gonna get over it. You gotta learn to live with it."

Let's back up a minute: Trailing 32–28 with 1:08 remaining, Murray and the Georgia offense had begun their game-winning quest from their own 15-yard line. It did not go to plan; a deep throw from Murray was

Georgia offensive lineman Kenarious Gates covers his face after a nail-biting loss to Alabama in the 2012 SEC Championship Game. In the words of quarterback Aaron Murray: "It's a game that will probably haunt me for the rest of my life." AP PHOTO/*ATLANTA JOURNAL-CONSTITUTION*, CURTIS COMPTON

deflected into the arms of Alabama cornerback Dee Milliner, and the Bulldogs quarterback walked off the field in disgust, his helmet in his hand. But the officials decided to review the play, and—as Georgia players knelt on the sideline, presumably praying for a favorable outcome—announced that the ball had hit the turf. Incomplete.

The dramatic turn of events left 'Bama vulnerable. Murray connected with tight end Arthur Lynch for 15 yards along the right sideline, with receiver Tavarres King for 23 yards down the middle, and Lynch again for 26 more yards down the middle.

Suddenly, Georgia had the ball at the Alabama 8-yard line.

"They're gonna get two throws to the end zone," remarked CBS commentator Gary Danielson. The clock hovered at 15 seconds while the chains moved.

Instead of spiking the football to give both teams a moment to breathe, Murray took the snap with 10 seconds left and looked down the field. Alabama's defense was flustered, while Georgia's offense appeared to have a matchup it liked.

Murray had his man, Mitchell, on a back-shoulder throw to the front pylon.

"Oh, it's a touchdown," Murray said a week after the game. "It's a 50-50 ball, and the guy [Alabama cornerback Milliner] is facing Malcolm and Malcolm's supposed to just go up and catch the ball."

The result would either be a game-winning pass or an incomplete pass that would stop the clock and allow the 'Dawgs at least one more play.

Unless . . .

The ball was tipped at the line of scrimmage. Blitzing Alabama linebacker C. J. Mosley had gotten his hand in the right place at the right moment. Instead of traveling toward the end zone, the football switched course to a different Georgia receiver, Chris Conley, who was 4 yards short of the goal line with two defenders covering him.

Conley snared the ball as he fell to the turf. A brief moment passed as everyone processed the gravity of the play: Georgia had no time-outs, and it did not have time to snap the ball again. The Bulldogs—standing just feet from a winning touchdown—could only watch as the final seconds slipped away.

Both Murray and coach Mark Richt were frozen in the moment. The Georgia Dome was engulfed by screams and wails, the sounds of celebration and horror mingling and reverberating off its roof.

Three weeks after a wild loss to Johnny Manziel and Texas A&M, Alabama was headed to Miami for the BCS national championship game vs. Notre Dame.

Georgia had simply "run out of time," per Richt. It was headed to the Capital One Bowl.

Such was the thin line between a ring and a mid-tier bowl game. And the difference was not lost on Crimson Tide coach Nick Saban, who claimed, "I'm ready to have a heart attack here."

The Bulldogs had more alarming issues.

"It's a game that will probably haunt me the rest of my life, honestly," Murray said.

COMPLETE LIST OF
SEC CHAMPIONSHIP GAME RESULTS

1992
No. 2 Alabama 28, No. 12 Florida 21
Venue: Legion Field (Birmingham)
MVP: Antonio Langham, Alabama
Winning coach: Gene Stallings
Favorite: Alabama by 10

1993
No. 9 Florida 28, No. 16 Alabama 13
Venue: Legion Field (Birmingham)
MVP: Terry Dean, Florida
Winning coach: Steve Spurrier
Favorite: Florida by 4

1994
No. 6 Florida 24, No. 3 Alabama 23
Venue: Georgia Dome (Atlanta)
MVP: Ellis Johnson, Florida
Winning coach: Steve Spurrier
Favorite: Florida by 7

1995
No. 2 Florida 34, No. 23 Arkansas 3
Venue: Georgia Dome (Atlanta)
MVP: Danny Wuerffel, Florida
Winning coach: Steve Spurrier
Favorite: Florida by 24

1996
No. 4 Florida 45, No. 11 Alabama 30
Venue: Georgia Dome (Atlanta)
MVP: Danny Wuerffel, Florida
Winning coach: Steve Spurrier
Favorite: Florida by 14.5

1997
No. 3 Tennessee 30, No. 11 Auburn 29
Venue: Georgia Dome (Atlanta)
MVP: Peyton Manning, Tennessee
Winning coach: Phillip Fulmer
Favorite: Tennessee by 7

1998
No. 1 Tennessee 24, No. 23 Miss. St. 14
Venue: Georgia Dome (Atlanta)
MVP: Peerless Price, Tennessee
Winning coach: Phillip Fulmer
Favorite: Tennessee by 14

1999
No. 7 Alabama 34, No. 5 Florida 7
Venue: Georgia Dome (Atlanta)
MVP: Freddie Milons, Alabama
Winning coach: Mike DuBose
Favorite: Florida by 7

2000
No. 7 Florida 28, No. 18 Auburn 6
Venue: Georgia Dome (Atlanta)
MVP: Rex Grossman, Florida
Winning coach: Steve Spurrier
Favorite: Florida by 9.5

2001
No. 21 LSU 31, No. 2 Tennessee 20
Venue: Georgia Dome (Atlanta)
MVP: Matt Mauck, LSU
Winning coach: Nick Saban
Favorite: Tennessee by 7

2002
No. 4 Georgia 30, No. 22 Arkansas 3
Venue: Georgia Dome (Atlanta)
MVP: Musa Smith, Georgia
Winning coach: Mark Richt
Favorite: Georgia by 8

2003
No. 3 LSU 34, No. 5 Georgia 13
Venue: Georgia Dome (Atlanta)
MVP: Justin Vincent, LSU
Winning coach: Nick Saban
Favorite: LSU by 3

2004
No. 3 Auburn 38, No. 15 Tennessee 28
Venue: Georgia Dome (Atlanta)
MVP: Jason Campbell, Auburn
Winning coach: Tommy Tuberville
Favorite: Auburn by 14.5

2005
No. 13 Georgia 34, No. 3 LSU 14
Venue: Georgia Dome (Atlanta)
MVP: D. J. Shockley, Georgia
Winning coach: Mark Richt
Favorite: LSU by 2.5

2006
No. 4 Florida 38, No. 8 Arkansas 28
Venue: Georgia Dome (Atlanta)
MVP: Percy Harvin, Florida
Winning coach: Urban Meyer
Favorite: Florida by 3

2007
No. 5 LSU 21, No. 14 Tennessee 14
Venue: Georgia Dome (Atlanta)
MVP: Ryan Perrilloux, LSU
Winning coach: Les Miles
Favorite: LSU by 7

2008
No. 2 Florida 31, No. 1 Alabama 20
Venue: Georgia Dome (Atlanta)
MVP: Tim Tebow, Florida
Winning coach: Urban Meyer
Favorite: Florida by 10

2009
No. 2 Alabama 32, No. 1 Florida 13
Venue: Georgia Dome (Atlanta)
MVP: Greg McElroy, Alabama
Winning coach: Nick Saban
Favorite: Florida by 5

2010
No. 2 Auburn 56, No. 18 South Carolina 17
Venue: Georgia Dome (Atlanta)
MVP: Cam Newton, Auburn
Winning coach: Gene Chizik
Favorite: Auburn by 3.5

2011
No. 1 LSU 42, No. 16 Georgia 10
Venue: Georgia Dome (Atlanta)
MVP: Tyrann Mathieu, LSU
Winning coach: Les Miles
Favorite: LSU by 12.5

2012
No. 2 Alabama 32, No. 3 Georgia 28
Venue: Georgia Dome (Atlanta)
MVP: Eddie Lacy, Alabama
Winning coach: Nick Saban
Favorite: Alabama by 7.5

2013
No. 3 Auburn 59, No. 5 Missouri 42
Venue: Georgia Dome (Atlanta)
MVP: Tre Mason, Auburn
Winning coach: Gus Malzahn
Favorite: Missouri by 2

2014
No. 1 Alabama 42, No. 14 Missouri 13
Venue: Georgia Dome (Atlanta)
MVP: Blake Sims, Alabama
Winning coach: Nick Saban
Favorite: Alabama by 14.5

2015
No. 2 Alabama 29, No. 18 Florida 15
Venue: Georgia Dome (Atlanta)
MVP: Derrick Henry, Alabama
Winning coach: Nick Saban
Favorite: Alabama by 17

2016
No. 1 Alabama 54, No. 15 Florida 16
Venue: Georgia Dome (Atlanta)
MVP: Reuben Foster, Alabama
Winning coach: Nick Saban
Favorite: Alabama by 24

2017
No. 6 Georgia 28, No. 4 Auburn 7
Venue: Mercedes-Benz Stadium (Atlanta)
MVP: Roquan Smith, Georgia
Winning coach: Kirby Smart
Favorite: Georgia by 1.5

PART 6: CHAMPIONSHIP MOMENTS

As the joke goes, Alabama football has won nearly as many national titles as it has conjured out of thin air.

At the end of Bear Bryant's career, the Tide officially claimed only six national titles, all of which came under Bryant. But that changed in the mid-'80s, when sports information director Wayne Atcheson decided to dish out credit for "championship" teams from 1925, 1926, 1930, 1934, and 1941.

Fans across the country have long busted the Tide's chops for its dubious title claims, including one on behalf of the two-loss '41 team—ranked No. 1 by just one soon-defunct selector (Houlgate)—that was supposedly superior to an undefeated Minnesota squad.

Held up against Notre Dame's standard of recognizing only consensus titles, 'Bama looks a little foolish, sure.

But it's not alone in the SEC. There's Tennessee's particularly head-scratching assertion that it won the 1967 national championship with a 9–2 record. And then there's Kentucky's claim that it won the 1950 title under Bryant, that title being a No. 1 spot in Jeff Sagarin's retroactive rankings four decades later. (The Wildcats have since commissioned a large championship trophy and placed it in one of their athletic buildings.)

In all, there are 34 national championships claimed by schools that represented the SEC during those championship seasons, and 39 if you include representatives of the Southern Intercollegiate Athletic Association (Georgia Tech in 1917 and 1928) and the Southern Conference (Alabama in '25, '26, and '30).

This chapter is a closer look at how some of those less-dubious titles came to be.

1929 ROSE BOWL: GEORGIA TECH VS. CALIFORNIA

Before the advent of TV, college football fans who could not score tickets to the Rose Bowl were forced to sit at home and wait for the details, typically via the local newspaper. What they got on the morning of January 2, 1929, was the stunning proclamation that "another tragic figure was added to the Hall of Goats."

Seventy thousand people had been on hand in Pasadena to watch California take on Georgia Tech. With the score 0–0 in the first half, Cal was deep in Georgia Tech territory before a failed fourth-down conversion turned the ball over.

On the first play of the ensuing drive, Tech back "Stumpy" Thomason fumbled near the 25-yard line. A California lineman named Roy Riegels grabbed the ball. Golden Bears fans screamed in delight. Then they screamed in horror.

Riegels had "whipped about-face," per the *Chicago Tribune*'s account, and begun running in the wrong direction.

"I started to turn to my left toward Tech's goal," he said postgame. "Somebody shoved me and I bounded right off into a tackler. In pivoting to get away from him, I completely lost my bearings."

The chase was on, just not the chase Riegels thought it was.

"Centers aren't supposed to be the fastest of runners," the *Tribune* report read. "But Riegels was grasping at the stuff of which heroes are made. He ran like one possessed."

Benny Lom, Cal's fastest player, sprinted after his teammate and caught up with him near the end zone, but a wall of Georgia Tech players smothered them inches from the goal line. In an era when field position was paramount, the Golden Bears decided to kick it away on first down.

Roy "Wrong Way" Riegels runs the wrong direction after scooping up a fumble during the 1929 Rose Bowl. His gaffe was highly publicized, and he later counseled young players who repeated his mistake. AP PHOTO

Naturally, Riegels was the long snapper and Lom was the punter. Georgia Tech blocked the kick for a safety and a 2–0 lead.

Labeled "a dejected, pitiful figure," Riegels left the game for the remainder of the first half.

In the second he returned to try and help the Golden Bears overcome his blunder. But Georgia Tech scored a touchdown to make it 8–0, and held on for an 8–7 victory, with Riegels's ill-fated dash leading to the difference on the scoreboard.

Back in 1929, the Rose Bowl was the only postseason game, and there was not a prominent pro football league. Riegels's gaffe was *the* play of the football season.

Dubbed "Wrong Way" Riegels, he received plenty of messages via mail afterward, including at least one marriage proposal. Other requests included his sponsorship of upside-down cakes and a "backward walkathon."

Over the years, Riegels learned to embrace the incident. Alongside Lom, he was named an honorary Yellow Jacket by the Georgia Tech Alumni Club in the mid-'60s, and the Rose Bowl inducted him into its Hall of Fame in 1991.

Following his playing career, he coached at Cal, served as an officer in the Armed Air Forces in World War II, and ran an agricultural chemicals company in Northern California. He reached out to other football players who made the same silly mistake he had, including Minnesota Vikings defensive lineman Jim Marshall, whose wrong-way run was—and still is—the most famous of its kind in NFL history.

In 1957 Riegels wrote to a high-school player in Southern California who had cost his team an important game with a dash in the wrong direction.

"For many years I've had to go along and laugh whenever my wrong-way run was brought up, even though I've grown tired listening and reading about it," Riegels wrote. "But it certainly wasn't the most serious thing in the world. I regretted doing it, even as you do, but you'll get over it."

1935 ROSE BOWL: ALABAMA VS. STANFORD

Long before "We want 'Bama!" there was "We want Minnesota!"

The Crimson Tide had won two Rose Bowls and three national titles by the 1934 season, but that dominance failed to impress the West Coast. When Stanford received a bid to the Rose Bowl, fans had little interest in a game vs. Alabama; they instead shouted for a showdown with the mighty Golden Gophers of Minnesota.

They didn't get what they wanted. So when the Alabama team arrived in Pasadena, it was met with chants of "We want Minnesota!"

Starting end Paul "Bear" Bryant said the incident "riled us up more than somewhat," but 'Bama had more to worry about than some annoying fans. Stanford had allowed just two touchdowns all season, and Bryant was particularly "scared" by 6-foot-4, 250-pound tackle Horse Reynolds. On the offensive side, running back Bobby Grayson was drawing comparisons to Illinois legend Red Grange.

It was Grayson who scored the first touchdown of the afternoon, giving the Indians a 7–0 lead in front of a cardinal-tinged crowd.

As comedian Will Rogers put it later, the score was "like holding up a picture of Sherman's March to the Sea in front of them Alabama boys."

The Tide rallied to put up 22 points in the second quarter, capped by a 54-yard touchdown pass from Joe Riley to Don Hutson, a future Hall of Fame receiver who was so calm before the Rose Bowl he "could go to sleep on the bench," per Bryant.

That enthralling touchdown pass came by accident. Coach Frank Thomas did not want Smith to call a pass play until the Tide had moved past the Stanford 40-yard line. He sent in a substitute to tell Smith as much, but in those days, substitute players were not allowed to give messages to the quarterback until they'd been in the game for one play.

It was during that one-play gap that Smith dialed up the deep ball to Hutson.

"I could just hear those people in the stands," Thomas joked afterward, "saying, 'That Thomas, what a genius he is.'"

Stanford cut the deficit to 9 points in the third quarter, but Alabama responded with another bomb to Hutson, this time a 59-yarder from star halfback Dixie Howell.

The Crimson Tide had a 29–13 win. The *Tuscaloosa News* called it an "Amazing Aerial Display" and said Alabama was "acclaimed by all sides as the greatest team to ever represent the South and East in the Rose Bowl." The victory gave Alabama a shared national title with—you guessed it—Minnesota.

1943 ROSE BOWL: GEORGIA VS. UCLA

One year after the attack on Pearl Harbor forced the Rose Bowl to switch coasts to Durham, North Carolina, the "Granddaddy of Them All" returned to Pasadena, albeit with a few twists.

The United States had recently defeated Japan in the Battle of Midway, which hastened the end of the Pacific Theater and allowed Californians to breathe a little more easily. But travel restrictions kept most Georgia fans from making the trip when their Bulldogs were selected to face UCLA. A large contingent of military men filled the empty seats, and the traditional Tournament of Roses parade was cancelled.

LEGEND
DON HUTSON

Even as he worked his way toward All-America honors as the nation's best pass catcher, Don Hutson kept his sights on Major League Baseball. The NFL just wasn't sexy enough.

"They didn't even write about it in the newspapers," he said.

His high school basketball coach had forced him to play football as a senior. When he showed promise, a pool-hall owner in Hutson's hometown of Pine Bluff, Arkansas, helped him land a spot on Frank Thomas's football team at Alabama.

Two bum seasons in the Cincinnati Reds baseball organization—and a two-touchdown showing in Alabama's 1935 Rose Bowl victory—helped steer Hutson toward the gridiron career he kept trying to avoid.

The "Alabama Antelope" agreed to sign with the Green Bay Packers, and it was not long before he was the league's best player.

"He had all the moves," fellow Packers legend Tony Canadeo said. "He invented the moves."

The era's passing game was so undeveloped that simple changes—for example, turning Hutson into a "split end" by lining him up near the side-line—were extremely progressive in the 1930s. Hutson essentially created modern route-running, and coach Curly Lambeau aided his ascension by moving him from the defensive line to safety, thereby helping him avoid big hits on defense.

He had too many legendary moments to publish in this space, but here are a couple of the best:

In one game against the Detroit Lions, he caught four touchdown passes and kicked 5 extra points . . . in one quarter. His record of 29 points in a single period still stands more than seven decades later.

In another game against the Cleveland Rams, Hutson was running a crossing route in the back of the end zone when he decided to change directions. Instead of simply stopping and cutting, he grabbed the right goalpost and swung himself around it—both feet off the ground—before making a one-handed touchdown catch.

Hutson did not rewrite the record books; he wrote them.

His 488 career receptions were 298 ahead of the nearest challenger at the time of his retirement. His single-season record of 17 touchdown receptions stood for 42 years. His 99 career touchdown catches stood for 44.

Hutson led the NFL in receptions eight times, including five consecutive seasons. He led the league in receiving yards seven times, including four consecutive seasons. He led the league in touchdown receptions nine times, including five consecutive seasons. Those are all still NFL records. (He also intercepted 30 passes in his career.)

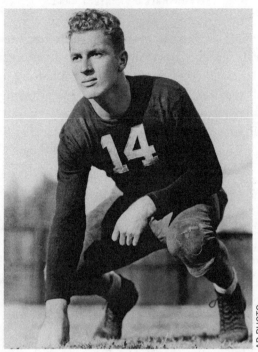

"He would glide downfield, leaning forward as if to steady himself close to the ground," Lambeau said. "Then, as suddenly as you gulp or blink an eye, he would feint one way and go the other, reach up like a dancer, gracefully squeeze the ball and leave the scene of the accident— the accident being the defensive backs who tangled their feet up and fell trying to cover him."

Of course, his time at Alabama was scintillating, too. Teammate Paul "Bear" Bryant knew he was watching an all-time great in Tuscaloosa.

"In all my life, I have never seen a better pass receiver," Bryant said. "He had great hands, great timing, and deceptive speed. He'd come off the line looking like he was running wide open, and just be cruising. Then, he'd really open up. He looked like he was gliding, and he'd reach for the ball at the exact moment it got there, like it was an apple from a tree."

Alabama coach Frank Thomas remembered a player who exhibited plenty of toughness to complement his graceful athleticism. There was an eerie calm about him, too.

"Hutson never tightened up," Thomas said. "He was as relaxed in the Rose Bowl as he was in practice."

Put simply by former Chicago Bears rival Clyde "Bulldog" Turner upon Hutson's death in 1997: "He was the best I've ever seen. I don't like to compare players then with players now. But he was head and shoulders above the ones in that era."

When Georgia arrived via train, the players had not showered or bathed in four days, and coach Wally Butts called a team meeting at the hotel before they could do so. After he told them to focus on the game—and not the distractions of Hollywood and its surrounding neighborhoods—he addressed the media.

"First of all," he said, as transcribed by the *Los Angeles Times*'s Paul Zimmerman, "I have a football coaching job to be done. But I also want *youall* to be my friends. I don't want to make anyone mad at me. I'm just a country boy in the big town for the first time and I want to do the right thing—just so I get a chance to coach my football team."

Per Zimmerman's account, Butts spent several days before the game worrying about his star player.

Heisman Trophy–winning halfback Frank Sinkwich—who had thrown for 1,392 yards during the regular season and graced dozens of magazine covers—injured one of his ankles during a scrimmage in Athens, and then hurt the other one during a scrimmage in Southern California.

Thankfully, his teammate, Charley Trippi, was also a future Hall of Fame selection. The first-year varsity player from Pittston, Pennsylvania, ignited the crowd with a booming punt early in the game. He passed and ran all over the Bruins, racking up 96 yards through the air and 130 on the ground. But coach Butts despised field goal attempts, and the 'Dawgs failed to capitalize on "at least five" scoring opportunities with the game tied 0–0, per the *Times*.

Special teams provided the necessary spark in the fourth quarter. Willard "Red" Boyd broke through the UCLA line and blocked a punt that went out of the end zone for a safety. Soon afterward, Clyde Erhart picked off a Bruins pass and returned it near the red zone. Trippi moved Georgia into position for the game-sealing touchdown, but could not punch it in.

In came Sinkwich, "obviously in great pain," and he barely managed to get the ball over the goal line. Georgia won, 9–0, dominating the box score in the process. The Bulldogs had outgained the Bruins, 379–157, and netted 24 first downs to the Bruins' 5.

Butts hurried to the locker room.

"Don't let those newspapermen in until I have had my shower," he instructed the army guards. "The perspiration is rolling off me like water after those terrific goal line stands by the Bruins."

Reality soon drowned out the postgame laughter. Fullback Jim Todd was the first player to get dressed. He said goodbye to his teammates and coaches and took a plane to Atlanta to join the armed forces. Assistant coach Howell Hollis left the next day for navy training camp.

And Trippi, the Rose Bowl star, was soon off to the air force.

"Others of the Georgians are headed for various camps," wrote the *Times*'s Paul Lowry, "leaving the memory of a glorious and hard victory over the battling Bruins behind them."

1951 VANDERBILT @ TENNESSEE

Long before the proliferation of bowl destinations and computer formulas, the Associated Press national championship was decided in December. There were plenty of other title selectors, but the AP poll swiftly became the king of such matters after its inception in 1935.

Sixteen years in, no SEC team had earned the No. 1 spot in the writers' final poll. Several teams had won championships given by other committees and analysts, but not the AP title.

So it was that No. 1-ranked Tennessee welcomed lowly Vanderbilt to Knoxville on December 1, 1951, for one of the most important games in conference history. Fans witnessed not only a classic contest, but also a near riot that would "grace" the front cover of the *Nashville Tennessean* the following morning.

The Vols were a powerhouse. They had just shut out Bear Bryant's No. 9-ranked Kentucky Wildcats, 28–0, to run their winning streak to 19 games. The Commodores . . . not so much. Vanderbilt had lost four of its seven SEC contests, and had failed to pass the 20-point mark in six consecutive contests.

Experts pegged the Vols as four-touchdown favorites.

On a dry day with the temperature in the mid-50s, Tennessee was well on its way to that mark, taking a 14–0 lead into halftime and scoring again in the third to make it 21–0.

LEGEND
FRANK SINKWICH

Frank Sinkwich's feet were so flat that the marine corps discharged him from basic training following his college football career. He had, as the *Miami Daily News* put it, "third-degree pancake too[t]sies."

He had arrived at Georgia in 1939 from Youngstown, Ohio, as one of the Bulldogs' most questionable prospects.

"Broad-bottomed, flat-footed, the all-around Sinkwich looked like little more than a candidate for oblivion when he first reported to Coach Butts," wrote John D. McCallum.

Early in his career, one Bulldogs coach gave him the following input: "You're not a good passer, and you'll never make All-American until you get that down pat. I don't believe you'll ever develop into a passer of any outstanding ability."

Sinkwich worked tirelessly to improve his arm and it paid off as he tore through the SEC during his junior and senior seasons. By then, "Flatfoot" had earned a new nickname: "Fireball."

In 1941 Georgia set the conference record for team yardage, racking up 429.5 per game. The following year, Sinkwich was the first player in college football history to amass 2,000 total yards of offense in a season. For his efforts, he became the first SEC player to win the Heisman Trophy, and was considered one of the most popular athletes in the country. The fact that he wore a mask on his face after breaking his jaw vs. Ole Miss only added to his legend.

Two postseason achievements stood out: In the 1942 Orange Bowl, Sinkwich dominated TCU with 382 combined yards and four total touchdowns. The next January, he overcame two bum ankles to score the game-clinching touchdown in the 1943 Rose Bowl.

The latter performance transcended the sports world during World War II.

"Feats such as Frank Sinkwich's in the Rose Bowl," wrote the *Cincinnati Enquirer*'s Bob Considine, "will be greeted as proof that, as a country, we can take it and dish it out in the face of adversity."

Following a memorable win over rival Georgia Tech in which Sinkwich fired three touchdown passes, the future NFL MVP had a question for the same Georgia staff member who had earlier doubted his aerial aptitude.

"Hey, coacher," he said, "am I an All-American passer now?"

LEGEND
CHARLEY TRIPPI

Following an excellent Rose Bowl performance in 1943, Georgia star Charley Trippi left football to serve in the air force. What happened between then and the moment he returned to Athens two years later was fodder for a heated national discussion.

Many people had questions about Trippi's discharge from active duty, which came after a pair of Georgia senators—Walter F. George and R. B. Russell—held a private meeting with Robert Patterson, the national secretary of war.

Trippi, who admittedly "never held a rifle" during his time in the armed forces—instead playing in exhibition football games as entertainment for the troops—waltzed back to the Peach State, the beneficiary of a sudden "surplus and hardship" exception.

Word flew that Trippi had turned down a $17,000 professional football offer in favor of a financial agreement with the University of Georgia, which was allegedly providing the junior "a modest salary plus incidentals" as compensation for his decision to return to school.

"We wouldn't know anything about such rumors," wrote the *Nashville Tennessean*'s William Tucker, "but after you talk to Trippi and meet his lovely wife and child, the stories seem unimportant. He is handsome Italian stock, modest as they come and an inspiration to every boy who plays with him. And when he tucks that ball under his arm he goes like a flying mouse out of the underworld."

Georgia had gone to extreme lengths to bring back its former star, and Trippi repaid his school handsomely.

In 1946 he captained Georgia to its first perfect season in 50 years, earning the Maxwell Award and finishing as first runner-up in the Heisman Trophy race. The Bulldogs were awarded the second national title of Trippi's career, and he parlayed that immense success into a $100,000 contract with the NFL's Chicago Cardinals.

The typically hapless Cardinals won the league championship during Trippi's rookie season, and he spent seven more years rewriting the team record book. A member of both the College Football Hall of Fame and Pro Football Hall of Fame by age 47, Trippi served as an assistant coach in Chicago before entering the real-estate world.

As of early 2018, he was still living in Athens with his wife, Peggy, at the age of 96.

"If I had to do it over," he said, "I'd concentrate more on real estate than football."

But the Vols were nearly undone by Commodores quarterback Bill Wade, who unleashed one of the most impressive aerial assaults the league had ever witnessed. Wade (16-of-24 for 251 yards on the afternoon) fired "bullet-like passes" to set up three Vandy touchdowns within an eight-minute stretch, and the 'Dores cut their deficit to 21–20 in front of a shocked homecoming crowd of 45,000 at Shields-Watkins Field.

Tennessee, "infuriated" by the turn of events, drove 71 yards for a crucial score, with Hal Payne punching in his second touchdown of the day. But Wade was not done. He completed four passes to move Vandy from its own 38-yard line to the Tennessee 4, and halfback Roy Duncan scored to again cut the deficit to 1 point.

Wade got one more chance with the football, and the Tennessee faithful feared the worst.

"If you'd have packed [the tension] in a Commodores uniform," reported the *Tennessean*, "the uniform would have stood up and slapped the dopesters with a pigskin."

But the Vols regained possession of the football at the Vandy 23-yard line and put home another touchdown in the closing seconds. That's when the fight began. Members of both teams began throwing punches, and a conglomerate of police officers, coaches, and fans stormed the field to break up the gridiron brawl.

Several reports did not even mention the free-for-all at the end of the game. National accounts focused on Wade and his resilient Vanderbilt teammates, who were welcomed back to Nashville like conquering heroes.

"A football team slated for slaughter rose up and poked the butcher in the nose yesterday in Knoxville," reported the *Tennessean*. "If the Commodores ever won a moral victory, they did it in UT stadium."

Added a Vandy student: "Maybe they call it a Tennessee win. But they're all wet. It just looks that way in the scorebook. It's a real victory from where we stand."

1960 SUGAR BOWL: OLE MISS VS. LSU

When LSU's Billy Cannon ran back his legendary Halloween punt return in 1959, it seemed Ole Miss would need to wait a full year to have its revenge for its dramatic 7–3 loss.

In November, Sugar Bowl president George Schneider expressed doubt that he could convince both teams to come to New Orleans for a rematch.

But No. 3-ranked Louisiana State soon accepted a Sugar Bowl bid, passing on other prominent options. One week later, No. 2-ranked Mississippi closed its regular season with a win in the Egg Bowl and accepted the bowl's other invitation.

Suddenly, LSU was a 7-point underdog in its own backyard, to a team that it had already defeated.

Much had changed since Cannon's touchdown in Oxford. The Tigers had slipped up at Tennessee one week after their monumental win, and several players were now either too injured to play or severely limited. Meanwhile, Ole Miss was playing excellent football. The Rebels had allowed just three touchdowns all season, and had outscored opponents 137–7 since losing to their hated SEC rivals.

Much like Halloween night, the weather was not cooperating. Tulane Stadium was cold, windy, and wet.

But "there were two distinct differences between today's game and that Halloweenish encounter," reported the *Jackson Clarion-Ledger*. "Some 20,000 more persons saw this one, and Ole Miss didn't lose."

Rebels coach Johnny Vaught, who had adopted a conservative game plan in the first game after taking a 3–0 lead, opened up his playbook. There were no more first-down punts, and the defense dismissed the Tigers' passing threat by matching up man to man across the formation.

Key LSU halfback Johnny Robinson had a fractured hand. He tried to play but exited the game soon after it kicked off. Fellow injured halfback Wendell Harris missed the contest entirely. That meant it was up to Cannon, the Heisman Trophy winner, to move the offense.

He did manage to move it . . . backwards. Ole Miss held Cannon to minus-3 rushing yards in the first half, and 8 yards overall. The Tigers only got as far as the Rebels 38-yard line, and that was after the game was out of reach.

All-America fullback Charlie Flowers bulldozed the LSU line with tough runs, allowing his teammates some breathing room to pass on the muddy turf.

LEGEND
ROBERT NEYLAND

The most successful defensive coach in SEC history learned a thing or two from the US Army.

Brigadier General Robert Reese Neyland had three different coaching stints in Knoxville, and all three meant hell for opposing offenses. Neyland, a champion of players' speed over brute strength, set several marks that will likely never be broken.

Between 1938 and 1939, his Vols shut out 17 consecutive opponents, and the '39 team was the last college football squad to not allow a single point during the regular season. In all, 112 of his Tennessee-record 173 wins came via shutout.

Much as he helped design and build bases in the China-Burma-India theater during World War II, he designed and built impenetrable football defenses.

Neyland is widely credited as the first coach to embrace film study, and he was always looking for an edge (sideline telephones, low-top shoes, lightweight pads, etc.) where rivals were not. His list of "Game Maxims" is still posted in the Tennessee locker room. A natural teacher, his coaching tree—which included Georgia Tech's Bobby Dodd—extended to as many as 90 pupils across the country at its peak, and as many as 175 of his former players were also active coaches at one point in time.

Born in 1892 in Greenville, Texas, Neyland (pronounced "KNEE-land") is recognized as one of the most accomplished athletes in the history of the US Military Academy at West Point. He won the academy's prestigious heavyweight boxing championship three times, won 35 games as a baseball pitcher, and contributed to an undefeated season as an end on the football team.

His career at Tennessee began innocuously as the captain in charge of the university's ROTC program and an assistant on the football field. By the following year, 1926, he was the head coach.

"I tried to get myself an ROTC job where I could do a little football coaching and experiment and see whether or not there was any sense to what I had dreamed up," he said. "That's actually how I got interested in it, and just like anything else you get your teeth into, you don't seem to be able to let go."

The army called him away twice, but Neyland made the most of his three terms with the Vols. He coached them to seven conference championships and four national titles, the last of which was awarded by the Associated Press—a first for an SEC team—in 1951.

Failing health booted him from coaching after the 1953 Cotton Bowl, and the same kidney and liver ailments led to his death nine years later.

He lives on through the Volunteers' current home venue. But he's more than a namesake; he used his civil engineering expertise to help expand the building capacity from 3,200 to 51,000 during his lifetime, and drew expansion plans that the university has followed over the years. Now 100,000 fans show up on Saturdays to watch Tennessee play football at Neyland Stadium.

Just before halftime, Rebels star Jake Gibbs—an All-American third baseman and all-SEC quarterback—dropped back to his left, whirled around near midfield, and launched a perfect pass to Cowboy Woodruff at the 10-yard line. Woodruff scampered into the end zone and tossed the ball back over his head in celebration.

Fellow All-SEC player Bobby Ray Franklin threw two more touchdown passes in the second half and was voted the game's most outstanding player in a dominant 21–0 victory.

"Some say Louisiana State didn't really want to come to this year's Sugar Bowl Classic," wrote Tommy Fitzgerald of the *Miami News*. "And there's some doubt among statisticians today that they did."

1966 ORANGE BOWL: ALABAMA VS. NEBRASKA

If Alabama fans saw Steve Sloan on the field, they knew Joe Namath was either hurt or deep in the doghouse. Sloan, a backup quarterback who filled in whenever Namath took a leave of absence, saw nearly as much playing time as Namath did during 1963 and 1964.

He led the Crimson Tide to a Sugar Bowl victory after Namath was suspended for "an infraction of training rules" and forced to take an early winter vacation in '63. Then, he guided 'Bama to several wins during an undefeated national championship season in '64 while the future "Broadway Joe" was out injured.

By the autumn of '65, Sloan—heavily involved in the Fellowship of Christian Athletes and known as "Smiler" for his upbeat nature—had the quarterback job to himself, and Bear Bryant was just fine with that.

"He was my kind of player," Bryant said later. "I couldn't have been closer to him if he had been my own son."

Alabama wasn't perfect that season, but New Year's Day madness put them in position to win a second straight national title. The Associated Press, which had long decided its champion before bowl season, had made the decision to delay until after January 1, and the switch proved fortuitous; both No. 1 Michigan State and No. 2 Arkansas fell, leaving No. 3 Nebraska and No. 4 Alabama to effectively decide the champion in the Orange Bowl.

'Bama had lost its season opener by one point to Georgia, and then tied Tennessee four weeks later. Now, the Tide was shockingly in position to win another title.

Bryant gave Sloan a message: "I want you to play all night as if we're behind."

The Tide dominated the football, running twice as many plays as the Huskers (86 to 43). It wasn't a run-heavy game plan, either; Sloan—battling bruised ribs—and receiver Ray Perkins lit up Nebraska through the air as 'Bama grabbed a 24–7 first-half lead and put away the Huskers in the third quarter for a 39–28 win that wasn't as close as the scoreboard suggested.

"No Bear Bryant team ever enjoyed itself more," John D. McCallum wrote. "They played with unrestrained joy. The backs exploded into the line like nitroglycerin, Sloan's bombs were on target, Perkins' hands were like suction cups . . . and when they finished totaling up the stats, it was revealed that Alabama gained more ground running the ball in the fourth quarter than Nebraska did the entire game."

Sloan had replaced Namath one last time—in the Orange Bowl record book. His 20 completions bested Namath's 18 the previous January, and he also broke Frank Broyles's passing mark with 296 yards against Nebraska.

The winning locker room was "wildly jubilant," per the *Anniston Star*.

"I don't know what it takes to be number one," Bryant said. "But with everyone getting beat today, I guess we're it."

1979 SUGAR BOWL: ALABAMA VS. PENN STATE

In the moments before No. 1 Penn State clashed with No. 2 Alabama in the 1979 Sugar Bowl, two things stuck out about Bear Bryant: First, he was not wearing his trademark fedora. Second, he was singing.

The hat was easy to explain ("He is too much of a gentleman to wear it inside," the public-address announcer told the crowd at the Louisiana Superdome). But . . . a vocal performance? Really?

"I don't know what he was singing, but when we heard him, we knew he was loose," linebacker Barry Krauss said. "And that made us loose. And you better believe that I wasn't going to ask him to name that tune."

LEGEND
JOHNNY VAUGHT

Ole Miss rarely won before Johnny Vaught showed up, and it hasn't done much winning since he left.

The Texas native, TCU All-American, and electric appliance salesman served as a lieutenant commander during World War II and then got a job on Red Drew's staff at Ole Miss. When Drew ditched town for Alabama, the leadership at Mississippi liked Vaught enough to keep him on as head coach.

He set to work building an offense around star passer Charlie Conerly. A firm believer in the split T offense, Vaught shelved his pride, scrapped that formation, and shifted to an adapted version of Notre Dame's shift-and-box. That allowed Conerly—an über-fit marine with a big arm who "ran like a duck and had less foot speed than a pregnant woodchuck," per John D. McCallum—to play tailback on both sides of the formation.

The new offense set several school records and powered Ole Miss to its first-ever SEC championship, which doubled as the first-ever meaningful title in the history of the 53-year-old program.

When Conerly left for the NFL, Vaught introduced his preferred split T formation, which eventually became a sensation. Ole Miss won two more conference titles in '54 and '55 (Vaught won six in his career), and then won the first of its three national titles in 1959 after beating rival LSU 21–0 in the Sugar Bowl.

In the words of McCallum, Vaught "was a burly, level-eyed hardworking man . . . who had the weathered look of a telephone lineman and the calm, authoritative eye of an old-time police captain. To borrow a Mississippi expression, he knew he could hit the center of a spittoon every time."

He refused to recruit married men, and forced players who owned automobiles to leave the cars at home. Rebels attended study halls Monday through Thursday, eventually building a better collective grade-point average than the rest of the university's male students.

During the height of desegregation tension in the early '60s, president John F. Kennedy made a personal call to Vaught's office, urging him to help keep campus "calm." The Rebels were at the peak of their football powers, and Vaught saw his team as an antidote to the political firestorm around him.

"I think the football team was a stabilizing factor for the state, for the university, and for the alumni," he said later. "I don't know what would have happened if we lost."

Vaught suffered a heart attack in 1970 and decided to step away from the game. But he returned three years later—taking over for Frank

Manning "Bruiser" Kinard, his former halfback—to salvage the Rebels' nosediving football reputation. He coached Ole Miss to a 5–3 record that year, including an upset win over No. 16 Tennessee, and then retired for good.

Mississippi has not won another SEC title since, and Vaught's 190–61–12 career record still stands head and shoulders above any other coach who's come through Oxford.

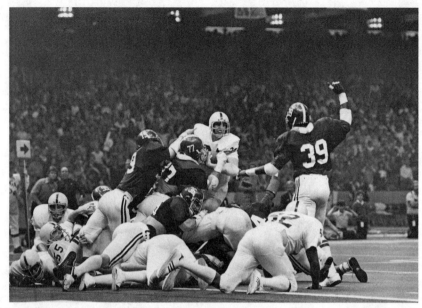

Trailing 14–7 and facing 4th-and-goal from the half-yard line, Penn State running back Matt Guhey hurls himself into a wall of Alabama defenders. He didn't manage to score on the play, but Penn State was not done. AP PHOTO

Alabama was in search of its fifth national title under Bryant, while Penn State was still looking for its first under any coach. In many analysts' minds, Joe Paterno—who had accepted an offer from the NFL's Boston Patriots six years earlier before changing his mind—was waiting to win a title before leaving Happy Valley. Win or lose, the New York Giants had been dogged in their attempts to convince Paterno to head east.

And for good reason: Penn State had been one of the most dominant teams of the 1970s. Four times, Paterno had finished with a perfect regular-season record, but the first three were not enough to secure a championship trophy. The fourth led to a matchup against the Crimson Tide on New Year's Day '79.

Paterno's top-ranked Nittany Lions had not lost in 19 games. Quarterback Chuck Fusina was "the best passer I've ever had," the coach said. Meanwhile, the Alabama defense was statistically one of the sketchiest of Bryant's 21-year Crimson Tide career. Injuries had slowed the secondary's progress, and the pass rush could not necessarily be counted on to reach Fusina.

All of that quickly went out the window.

Following kickoff, Penn State's passing offense was so ineffective that Alabama defensive coordinator Ken Donahue must have felt as if he were dreaming. Donahue had concocted the perfect game plan—a disorienting combination of "stunting, blitzing, looping"—to combat the Nittany Lions, who finished the first half with just 21 yards of offense. Alabama sacked Fusina five times for minus-70 yards and intercepted four of his passes over the course of the afternoon.

Penn State entered the game allowing fewer than 60 rushing yards per contest, but had not faced the patented 'Bama wishbone offense in four seasons. Tide running back Tony Nathan kept finding room along the fringes of the Penn State defensive line. He took several tosses for positive gains, finishing the game with 127 yards.

The scoreboard, however, was not reflecting the one-sided box score.

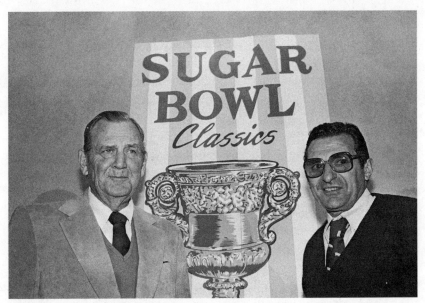

Alabama's Bear Bryant and Penn State's Joe Paterno pose for a promotional photo before the 1979 Sugar Bowl. Rumors swirled that Paterno was headed for the NFL, but he remained in Happy Valley for three-plus more decades. AP PHOTO

Alabama quarterback Jeff Rutledge found a diving Bruce Bolton for a 30-yard touchdown in the closing seconds of the first half, but Penn State eventually responded in the third quarter with a tying touchdown pass from Fusina to Scott Fitzkee, who made a sprawling catch in the back of the end zone and somehow avoided injuring himself on a nearby golf cart.

With the score knotted 7–7, the Nittany Lions forced the Tide into a three-and-out, and—statistics be damned—suddenly had a chance to take the lead in the fourth.

It was a moment Penn State needed to take advantage of, but Alabama shut the door. Donahue dialed up a safety blitz, and Murray Legg tracked down Fusina well behind the line of scrimmage for a momentous sack. On the ensuing punt, 'Bama returner Lou Ikner caught the kick, found breathing room on the left sideline, and then weaved all the way down to the Penn State 11-yard line.

On third-and-7, Rutledge bounced off a diving Penn State defender and pitched left to running back Major Ogilvie, who crashed into the end zone for a 14–7 lead.

Two turnovers set up a wild finish. Deep in Alabama territory, Fusina tossed an interception into triple coverage. On the next play, Rutledge made an awkward play on the option and tossed the football off Nathan, who had turned away to block. Penn State recovered at the 19.

Soon, the Nittany Lions were at the 1-yard line needing a touchdown to tie the game.

On third down, running back Matt Suhey took a handoff and attempted to dive over the defensive front. But Alabama met him at the line of scrimmage and held him out of the end zone. On fourth down, from the half-yard line, reserve back Mike Guman hurled himself into the fray and ran into a wall of crimson.

That wall was mostly Krauss, a linebacker whose job was to meet the ballcarrier in the air as his teammates submarined underneath. He pinched a neck nerve and briefly lost consciousness, but the crowd noise told him his attempt to stuff Guman had been successful.

"He didn't make it!" ABC commentator Keith Jackson yelled as the Superdome hit full volume.

With a little more than four minutes remaining, 'Bama was not yet in the clear. The Tide was forced to punt from their own end zone, and disaster struck again. A poor long snap forced punter Woody Umphrey to rush his kick, which took an ugly path out of bounds near the Alabama 20-yard line.

This time, though, PSU had made a crucial mistake. An unknown player—Paterno refused to name him after the game—had been in the wrong place at the wrong time, resulting in a 12-men-on-the-field penalty that gave Alabama 15 yards and a fresh set of downs.

Able to run more time off the clock and eventually pin Penn State back in its own territory with fewer than three minutes to go, Alabama's red-hot defense was in great position to seal the game.

Fusina completed a few passes, but his fourth-down throw near midfield fell incomplete, and Alabama later picked off his last-gasp heave. The Crimson Tide was—for the fifth time under Bear Bryant—the national champion.

The only consolation for Penn State was that Paterno was not headed to the NFL.

He effectively turned down the Giants in the postgame locker room, stating, "I'm going to be around awhile."

Bryant, armed with a Coke and a cigarette, proclaimed that his team could have beaten anyone in the country with such a performance. He could not recall being prouder of any other Alabama squad in his two-decades-plus of duty on the Crimson Tide sideline.

Minutes earlier, he had been walking around the Superdome when a photographer called out to the 65-year-old coach, urging him to smile.

"I'm too happy to smile," he said. "I want to cry."

1981 SUGAR BOWL: GEORGIA VS. NOTRE DAME

As the biggest game of his life approached, Georgia coach Vince Dooley found himself asking his team for forgiveness. The Auburn alum and former roommate of Alabama governor Fob James had reportedly been offered a $1 million contract to leave his undefeated Bulldogs and begin anew with the Tigers.

Dooley's noncommittal statements to reporters intensified the rumors. It got to the point where his team—ranked No. 1 in the country—began wondering why he didn't just leave already.

The coach eventually turned down Auburn, but was forced to hold a special meeting with his players.

"Well, will you take me back?" he asked.

Following a long pause, he asked again. The players began to nod. Dooley was staying, and the Bulldogs still had a Sugar Bowl date with Notre Dame to prepare for.

Notre Dame's Dan Devine, coaching the final game of his career, attempted to shock the 'Dawgs out of the gate. The Fighting Irish opened the contest with freshman Blair Kiel at quarterback—senior Mike Courey was expected to start—and Kiel launched a skyscraping pass down the left sideline.

Red-clad fans breathed a sigh of relief after the football fell through the hands of receiver Tony Hunter. But there was soon a much more stressful problem to deal with.

Stud Bulldogs freshman Herschel Walker, who entered the game with more than 1,600 yards and 15 rushing touchdowns, slammed his left shoulder into a Notre Dame defender on Georgia's second play. The shoulder subluxated, partially popping out and then back in, and Walker was forced to the sideline.

Coach Vince Dooley said the team doctor was "very concerned."

"I was thinking this is not good," the coach said. "We had to find some way to win, but it didn't look good."

Once Walker's shoulder got the green light again, Georgia pretended as if nothing had happened. The freshman hauled 34 more carries—none for more than 23 yards—against a stingy Notre Dame defense. The only sign that he'd been hurt: he held the ball with his right arm instead of his left.

The 'Dawgs had no choice but to keep feeding Walker; their passing game was in disarray, as quarterback Buck Belue failed to record a single completion in the first 57 minutes against the Notre Dame defense.

"Those guys were so big, Buck couldn't see over the defense," receiver Lindsay Scott said.

A trio of early errors by Notre Dame kept Georgia off the hook. After posting a 3–0 lead, the Irish lined up for another field goal late in the first quarter. But Georgia freshman defensive back Terry Hoage shot through the middle of the formation, planted his foot on the back of a Fighting Irish player, and jumped to stuff the kick. Minutes later, the game was tied.

On the ensuing kickoff, two Irish returners failed to communicate over the crowd noise and allowed the football to drop to the turf inside the 5-yard line. Georgia's Steve Kelly tackled one of the returners out of the play, while his brother Bob Kelly, a senior, pounced on the ball. Walker needed just two plays to leap into the end zone—bum shoulder and all— for the game's first touchdown.

The final Irish blunder: fullback John Sweeney fumbled the ball deep inside his own territory, and Walker again capitalized with a 3-yard score to make it 17–3, Georgia, with 13:49 remaining in the first half.

From there, the Bulldogs offense disappeared. Georgia failed to pick up a single first down for the majority of the second half, leaving the 'Dawgs defense to hold on to its two-score lead for dear life. The D got some help from Irish kicker Harry Oliver, who missed two close-range field goals (from 30 yards and 38 yards), but a 1-yard touchdown run by Notre Dame's Phil Carter made it 17–10 with the third quarter coming to a close.

"We knew our offense was struggling," Georgia's Bob Kelly said many years later. "It was having a tough time. The sense of the defense was we can't let them score anymore. That's it. Period."

Defensively, the game came down to a fourth-and-1 at the Georgia 48. Kiel dropped back, but pass-rusher Jimmy Payne was all over him. The freshman quarterback quickly tossed the ball toward an unsuspecting receiver, and Georgia defensive back Scott Woerner snagged his second interception of the day.

On the ensuing Bulldogs drive, the offense faced third-and-7 with a little more than two minutes on the clock. Belue, 0-for-11 at that point, rolled right and finally hit a receiver, Amp Arnold, who picked up the game-clinching first down.

LEGEND

HERSCHEL WALKER

As the story goes, Herschel Walker's 50-yard touchdown was called back due to a clipping penalty. The star running back was so upset, he huddled up his teammates for an important message.

"If you're not going to block them," he said, "just get out of the way."

The offensive line at Johnson County (Georgia) High School got out of Walker's way and watched him run for more than 3,000 yards and 45 touchdowns to deliver the Trojans a state championship.

Born in Augusta and raised in Wrightsville, Walker was new to the spotlight; he had been an overweight child with a speech impediment.

"A lot of kids in my school at the time wouldn't give me the time of day," Walker said. "They wouldn't even play with me. For four years I never went out for recess . . . the teachers used to put me down. They didn't think that I could ever learn. So at one point in my life, enough was enough."

He began strength training and developed a passion for martial arts and football. The latter sport would pay much quicker dividends.

Walker's prep career at Johnson County High was legendary. Seemingly every major college program in the country arrived in Wrightsville to speak with him. Southern Cal, Notre Dame, and Clemson all wanted to check on the kid who had reportedly run a 9.5-second 100-yard dash and had thighs the size of bourbon barrels. Some recruiters stayed in town for a month or longer; a Georgia assistant actually moved into a Wrightsville house lent to him by a wealthy alumnus.

Skeptics wondered who had paid for Walker's $12,000 Pontiac Trans-Am. A local news station launched an investigation and determined it was Walker's father, though that announcement did little to calm the storm.

Forced to finally make a decision in April, the all-star prospect chose Georgia.

Walker, listed as fourth-string on the depth chart, checked into an early-season game at Tennessee and demolished Vols safety Bill Bates for an iconic first touchdown run ("My God," yelled play-by-play announcer Larry Munson, "a freshman!") that helped the 'Dawgs avoid a September upset. From then on, he was the Bulldogs' workhorse, racking up more than 1,600 yards and 15 touchdowns to become the first freshman in NCAA history to finish as high as third in the Heisman Trophy voting.

His encore: a 150-yard, two-touchdown MVP performance in the Sugar Bowl against Notre Dame, with almost every carry coming after badly injuring his left shoulder in the first quarter. He had essentially dragged Georgia to its first national title, and some began to wonder if the teenager might be the greatest running back to ever play college football. He was certainly one of the most physically imposing.

From a 1981 *New York Times* feature: "At 19, he dwarfs most of his teammates, muscles layered in great slabs and chunks, rump-size thighs, tight, 31-inch waist, chest and shoulders of a bull, 6 feet 2 inches and 220 pounds. He seems even bigger on one of the infrequent occasions when he loses his temper."

AP PHOTO/AL MESSERSCHMIDT

Two years and a few thousand yards later, the Heisman winner and All-American track-and-field star faced a mountain of controversy regarding his eligibility. Reports circulated that he had signed a contract with the upstart United States Football League. He denied the news, but he was lying.

Instead of chasing Tony Dorsett's all-time college rushing record (he was 823 yards away) and competing in the 1984 Summer Olympics, Walker had indeed put pen to paper with the New Jersey Generals. The deal was reportedly the sweetest in pro football history, worth $5 million over five years with a $1.5 million signing bonus. He would make about $300,000 more annually than Sweetness himself, Walter Payton.

Dooley called it a "mistake" and a "sad day for Georgia football." Walker asked his coach—and God—for forgiveness in a prepared statement. But he was gone, along with his SEC-record 5,259 career rushing yards and 49 touchdowns.

The USFL was not much more of a challenge than college ball. Walker won two rushing titles in his first three seasons, and his total of 2,411 in 1985 still stands as the single-season professional record across all leagues. He later made two consecutive Pro Bowls with the NFL's Dallas Cowboys, and served as the key piece in an infamous 1989 trade between the Cowboys and Minnesota Vikings that helped Dallas build its '90s dynasty.

Walker was a little more eccentric than your average running back. He once danced with the Fort Worth Ballet, and found time to compete in the two-man bobsled at the 1992 Winter Olympics, finishing seventh. Following 14 years of pro football, he worked his way up to a fifth-degree blackbelt in taekwondo, and eventually began a short mixed-martial arts career in 2010.

Five years later, he claimed he could still play football at the age of 53.

"I've gotta get out of the fighting first," he said after claiming he had recently run a 4.3-second 40-yard dash. "Once I get out of the MMA stuff, then I may go back and play. I want to be the George Foreman of football."

"I'm happy," Belue said afterward, trying his best not to linger on his rough outing. "I had rather complete zero passes and win than complete 50 and lose."

Georgia fans began crowding the sideline in anticipation of an all-time celebration. They poured onto the field as the clock hit all zeroes, turning the Superdome turf into the Red Sea.

President Jimmy Carter, a Georgia Tech alum, was supposed to deliver a postgame speech to the 'Dawgs, but the environment become so raucous that the Secret Service whisked Carter away. He later called Dooley to congratulate him on the victory.

Despite cries from Pittsburgh and Norman, Oklahoma, that Georgia had not faced impressive enough competition ("a pantywaist regular-season schedule," wrote Cox News Services), it was clear the Bulldogs—the nation's only undefeated major-college team—were about to win the school's first national championship.

Walker, on his way to a Hall of Fame career, had run for 150 yards with his busted shoulder to earn MVP honors.

His 'Dawgs had lost battles in several categories, total yards, first downs and time of possession among them. But they could care less. They were getting rings, after all.

"We've been that kind of a team," said Dooley, who would coach eight more seasons in Athens before retiring. "We prepare to be lucky. We prepare to take advantage of the breaks when they come."

1997 SUGAR BOWL: FLORIDA VS. FLORIDA STATE
Of course it was Florida State. It was always Florida State.

Steve Spurrier's Florida Gators had been one of the most successful teams of the 1990s, but had not been able to reach No. 1 at the end of the season. More often than not, that was due to Bobby Bowden and the hated Florida State Seminoles.

Spurrier's "Fun 'n' Gun" offense was set to finally conquer college football in 1996. Quarterback Danny Wuerffel was coming off an all-time great junior season. Receivers Ike Hilliard and Reidel Anthony were both All-Americans and future first-round draft picks, and running back Fred Taylor would go on to rush for more than 11,000 yards in the NFL.

Bitter rivals Bobby Bowden (left) and Steve Spurrier (right) convene after Spurrier's Gators earned their first-ever national championship. Earlier that season, Spurrier had called Bowden a "dirty" coach. AP PHOTO/DAVE MARTIN

Florida started 10–0, averaging 49.3 points per game and holding down the top spot in the country for eight consecutive weeks.

Then came a trip to Tallahassee to play No. 2-ranked Florida State on Thanksgiving weekend. Florida fell behind by 10 points in the fourth quarter, and a late rally came up short. Wuerffel was battered to the point that Spurrier sent film of the game to the NCAA and called Bowden a "dirty" coach. There was, of course, already a colorful history between the teams.

Over the previous four years, Florida had been given six chances to beat Florida State, but did so only once. The most excruciating result was 1994's "Choke at Doak," in which the Gators surrendered a 28-point lead in the final quarter to allow a tie. Bowden knew the wind would eventually blow in the other direction, and it seemed he'd rather play the Green Bay Packers than the Florida Gators (again) in the '97 Sugar Bowl.

"I don't want no more of them," he said after the November win. "Yeah, I'm a coward. Never said I wasn't."

The rematch happened, anyway, and Bowden's fears proved to be legitimate.

Spurrier helped keep the fierce FSU pass rush at bay by having his offense use a silent snap count, and Wuerffel hit Hilliard on a 9-yard touchdown pass on UF's first drive. That set the tone for a breakneck first half that ended with Florida ahead 24–17.

Key to the performance was Florida's shotgun offense, which Spurrier reluctantly leaned on after Wuerffel was sacked six times behind a beat-up offensive line in Tallahassee. It kept the senior clean in an SEC title game win vs. Alabama, and Spurrier decided to stick with it in New Orleans.

Through two quarters vs. Florida State, the shotgun had afforded Wuerffel enough space to complete several big passes between collisions with defenders.

"You beat on him and you beat on him like an old church bell," ABC's Keith Jackson remarked after Wuerffel's second touchdown toss. "Then he suddenly sticks it to you."

With a 24–20 lead seemingly slipping away in the third quarter, the Gators hit a new gear.

The defense held 'Noles running back Warrick Dunn at bay, and the offense began moving the football at will. Wuerffel threw a 7-yard score to Hilliard—the receiver's third touchdown of the game—and then ran in another score from 16 yards out before the quarter was over.

Running back Terry Jackson effectively ended the game with a 42-yard touchdown dash in the fourth. Florida was up 25 points, and Florida State was beginning to show signs of frustration. Three FSU penalties kept alive Florida's final scoring drive, and Spurrier stuck it to the 'Noles by crossing the 50-point threshold in garbage time.

The final: 52–20, Florida.

Due to a fortunate sequence of events to end the season—Michigan's defeat of Ohio State, Texas's defeat of Nebraska, and Ohio State's

Rose Bowl win over Arizona State—the Gators were likely to be named national champions for the first time.

Wuerffel had put the ideal finishing touch on a legendary season, finishing 18-of-34 for 306 yards and four total touchdowns. His teammates danced on the Superdome turf for at least 45 minutes after the final whistle.

Spurrier continued to bash Florida State's sportsmanship during postgame interviews, then showered and took his family back to their hotel suite. He cracked open a Coors Light and soaked in the moment.

"We wanted this one very, very badly," he said. "Golly, it's a thrill for Gators everywhere."

Back in the Superdome, Bowden was still upset he had been forced into another matchup with Florida.

"You can see why we didn't want to play them again, don't you?" he asked reporters. "Too good."

1999 FIESTA BOWL: TENNESSEE VS. FLORIDA STATE

The first edition of the Bowl Championship Series went over smoothly. Fears of wacky formulas and arbitrary selections were put aside and . . .

No, scratch that. It was a complete mess.

John Cooper, coach of No. 4-ranked Ohio State, called for a playoff. Kansas State president Jon Wefald complained—loudly—that his No. 3-ranked team was not only missing out on the championship game, but somehow being relegated to the Alamo Bowl. Bobby Bowden, coach of No. 2-ranked Florida State, had a golden ticket to Phoenix and even he had serious doubts about the process.

Put simply by a bummed-out Kansas State student: "Everybody's in shock. Everybody's dead."

The only thing universally agreed upon was that No. 1 Tennessee deserved to be in the title game.

Phillip Fulmer's Vols were 12–0 after dispatching Mississippi State in the SEC championship. Tennessee, having survived major scares against Syracuse, Florida, and Arkansas, was the closest thing the nation had to a team of destiny in '98.

Tennessee wide receiver Peerless Price sprints toward the end zone for a pivotal touchdown in the 1999 Fiesta Bowl. His score gave the Volunteers a 20–9 lead and put them on the cusp of a rare national title.
AP PHOTO/ERIC DRAPER

Peyton Manning was no longer in Knoxville, but Tee Martin had filled in admirably at quarterback. The Vols now leaned on a diverse stable of rushers and a suffocating defense that featured All-American middle linebacker Al Wilson.

UT was a 5.5-point underdog to Florida State, and had not won a national title in nearly five decades.

But Fulmer had done about as much winning as a nonchampion possibly could. He was 66–11 since taking over for the legendary Johnny Majors in the early '90s—his 85.7 was the highest winning percentage of any active coach—including 44–5 over his past four seasons. Rocky Top had been building up to this stage for quite some time.

"He'd been overshadowed by Florida and overshadowed by the conference," Bowden said of Fulmer during the lead-up to the game. "Then he won the conference championship [in 1997] and now he's going for the national championship. I would say he has arrived. He didn't arrive five years ago. He arrived now."

After all the BCS hoopla and consternation, the two teams selected to play for the championship played a sleepy first quarter.

It wasn't until Florida State safety Dexter Jackson—a future Super Bowl MVP—made a costly error that the game broke open. Jackson, attempting to block a chip-shot Tennessee field goal, crashed into kicker Jeff Hall. Instead of 3 points, the Vols got a new set of downs, and Martin found Shawn Bryson for a short touchdown pass that made it 7–0.

A few plays later, Seminoles quarterback Marcus Outzen made an ill-advised throw to the right sideline, where Vols cornerback Dwayne Goodrich snared the ball and returned it 54 yards to the end zone, where costumed Tennessee mascot Smokey lifted him off the ground with a hug.

The rout was not quite on, however.

Martin, seeing single coverage on an outside receiver, thought he might make it 21–0 with a throw deep down the middle. But he failed to account for safety Derrick Gibson, who made an easy interception and ran it back to the Tennessee 4-yard line. William McCray reached over the goal line on a third-down run, putting FSU on the scoreboard (though Sebastian Janikowski's extra-point attempt was partially blocked and bounced off the crossbar, no good).

Later in the quarter, Janikowski blasted a 34-yarder through the uprights to cut the Tennessee lead to 14–9.

Neither team scored in the third quarter, leaving Tennessee with an uneasy 5-point advantage entering the final period. The Vols were 0-for-8 on third downs, while the Seminoles were beginning to pick up a little steam on offense.

One man who had been relatively quiet was Peerless Price, a senior receiver from Dayton, Ohio, who had starred in the Vols' SEC championship game win and had 11 touchdowns on the season. If Tennessee were to have an iconic moment during the national title game, Price was probably the best bet to provide it.

On third-and-9 from the Tennessee 21-yard line, Price streaked down the right sideline as Martin dropped back. The quarterback slipped briefly, but regathered himself and tossed a high, arcing pass—a prayer, it seemed—in Price's direction.

ABC announcer Keith Jackson didn't even raise his voice as the ball soared through the air. The play seemed doomed to fail, another hopeless attempt from the hapless Vols O.

But just as it careened toward the ground, Price got a few inches of separation. He swooped underneath the ball at the last moment and snagged it.

"That ball going down the sidelines is . . . CAUGHT!" Jackson yelled in surprise.

Price outran his defender to the end zone for a 79-yard touchdown and a 20–9 lead.

With 9:17 remaining on the clock, Tennessee sensed its championship was near. Players hollered and jumped up and down on the sideline, imploring fans to bring the noise. When Outzen fumbled 20 seconds later, the stadium erupted. Tennessee tacked on a field goal to make it 23–9, and figured to coast to the finish line.

Florida State opted for a dramatic ending. The 'Noles punched in a touchdown with 3:42 remaining and nearly converted an onside kick. ABC announcer Bob Griese declared "ballgame" after Tennessee converted a fourth-and-1 at the Florida State 33-yard line, but the game still would not end. Travis Henry fumbled at the 10, giving the Seminoles one more shot.

Bowden's team needed to move 90 yards in 89 seconds. It got zero.

Outzen tossed a deep pass into double coverage, and it wound up in the hands of defensive back Steve Johnson.

The band launched into "Rocky Top." Tennessee had its first national title since 1951.

"People said all year we were a team of destiny," Fulmer said. "It wasn't always perfect. It wasn't always the prettiest, but they always found a way to get it done."

2004 SUGAR BOWL: LSU VS. OKLAHOMA

One man probably benefited more from BCS controversy than any other: Nick Saban.

The former Cleveland Browns defensive coordinator and Michigan State head coach left East Lansing at the turn of the millennium to become LSU's 30th head coach. Only one Tigers boss before him—Paul Dietzel in 1958—had won a national title, and the program had not secured a Top 10 finish in 13 years.

Saban, a defensive-minded, no-nonsense coach with an eye for detail, quickly moved LSU back into the national picture. Louisiana State won the Sugar Bowl in his second season, and he had a championship-caliber roster two years later in 2003.

Led by SEC Defensive Player of the Year Chad Lavalais and future NFL picks Marcus Spears, Corey Webster, and Marquise Hill, the Tigers

LSU coach Nick Saban throws his hands in the air after the clock hits 0:00 in the 2004 Sugar Bowl. The win marked his first national championship, and he would go on to win five more with Alabama. AP PHOTO/DAVE MARTIN

defense held six different opponents to single digits and keyed a 34–13 blowout of No. 5 Georgia in the conference championship game. There was a major roadblock for the 12–1 Tigers, however: they were stuck at No. 3 in both the AP and coaches' polls.

Cue the BCS's "finest" moment: the formula somehow bumped USC—No. 1 in both major polls—to No. 3, making room for LSU to squeeze into the national title game vs. Oklahoma.

This drew waves of criticism from around the country. Even LSU quarterback Matt Mauck called the situation "kind of messed up," while Saban said, "I don't think anyone will know who the legitimate national champion is."

USC blew out Michigan in their ensuing Rose Bowl matchup, meaning whoever won the LSU-Oklahoma Sugar Bowl matchup would most likely share the national title with Pete Carroll's Trojans.

The Tigers were ready for their close-up. Skyler Green and Justin Vincent both ran in touchdowns for a 14–7 lead before Spears—a defensive end—made the play of the game by returning Heisman Trophy winner Jason White's errant pass 20 yards for a score to make it 21–7. The Sooners eventually closed the gap to 21–14 with 11:01 remaining and had several chances to tie the game; none was more dramatic than a fourth-down pass that slipped past star receiver Mark Clayton's dive in the end zone.

But a last-gasp Oklahoma drive was quickly snuffed out by Spears and Co., and LSU claimed its first national title in 45 years.

2008 BCS NATIONAL CHAMPIONSHIP GAME: LSU VS. OHIO STATE

From the *Louisiana Gannett News* on November 24, 2007: "Not only did LSU's national championship hopes go out the window on a cold early evening in Baton Rouge, so did the legacy of a defense that was once considered one of the best in program history."

The college football world had no idea which teams would be in the national title game. But it knew one thing: LSU would not be involved.

Everyone had just witnessed the death knell of Les Miles's once-serious bid for a national title. For the second time that autumn, a No.

1-ranked LSU team had lost a three-overtime game. Those two losses meant the Tigers were done.

The Associated Press dropped them to No. 5. The coaches dropped them to No. 7. The all-important BCS standings listed them at No. 7, too.

In front of them: Missouri, West Virginia, Ohio State, Georgia, Kansas, and Virginia Tech.

Miles and the Tigers snuck in a comeback win against Tennessee in the SEC title game and then prayed for the best. As they flew back to Baton Rouge, they received score updates from the cockpit. Impossibly, unranked Pitt—a 28.5-point underdog—had knocked off No. 2 West Virginia in the Mountaineers' Big East finale. Then, news came through that No. 1 Missouri had dropped the Big 12 title game to Oklahoma.

The LSU plane "was bobbing around" in the air as players celebrated. Experts suddenly predicted that the Tigers would leapfrog Georgia, Kansas, and Virginia Tech—all of which sat out the weekend—and face Ohio State for the national championship.

They were right. The BCS slotted Ohio State No. 1 and LSU No. 2.

"LSU has a ticket to the title game," read an Associated Press report. "Everyone else has a pretty good gripe."

Adding to the drama, rumors had been flying all fall that Miles was leaving town to take the open job at Michigan, his alma mater. He had mostly pushed away that talk, but met with Michigan brass in the days after LSU's conference championship.

His explanation: he was simply helping his former school find a new coach. He himself was not a candidate.

None of this sat well with LSU, which had just lost Nick Saban in a surprise move to the NFL's Miami Dolphins three years earlier. But the page turned when Michigan hired West Virginia coach Rich Rodriguez on December 17, allowing Miles and the rest of Louisiana to breathe easy.

His team had gone from No. 7 to the favorite to win the national title, after all. The Tigers were given a 5.5-point advantage in Vegas, thanks in no small part to Florida's revelatory demolition of Ohio State the previous January. The Buckeyes were "perhaps the most maligned No. 1 team in recent memory," per ESPN, to the point that coach Jim Tressel gave his players 10-minute DVDs of various television pundits tearing them down.

Reporters peppered the Bucks with questions—both subtle and not so subtle—about LSU's perceived edge in athleticism.

"It's not all about the SEC speed," quarterback Todd Boeckman said. "I think we have guys that can run, too."

It was such an emphasized narrative that LSU got tired of hearing about it, as well.

"When people come up and try and get me to fall into the thing about Ohio State being slow and the SEC being really fast and how we're going to blow them out," Tigers wideout Early Doucet said, "I'm not buying into that."

Soon after kickoff, it seemed both players were right. Buckeyes running back Chris "Beanie" Wells blew past the LSU defense for a 65-yard touchdown run, and the Tigers offense failed to move the ball as Ohio State built a 10–0 first quarter lead.

Then, the media got its "told you so" moment. Well, lots of "told you so" moments.

Led by the accurate arm of Matt Flynn and the bruising running of Jacob Hester, the Tigers ripped off 24 unanswered points before halftime. Flynn capped two lengthy drives with touchdown passes, and Hester plowed into the end zone for a 1-yard touchdown as the LSU defense smothered Boeckman and the Bucks with its, well, SEC speed.

Not much changed in the second half. Flynn led a six-minute drive that Doucet finished by catching a pass near the line of scrimmage and slipping out of three Ohio State defenders' hands to slide into the end zone.

LSU's 21-point lead was cut to 14 on two separate occasions, but it never seemed in any real danger. Ohio State's last touchdown came in garbage time, making the final score—38–24—a little less ugly than the contest itself.

The Tigers were the first two-loss team to win a national title in 47 years.

"I have to give great credit to some divine intervention that allows us to be in this position," Miles said.

Chants of "SEC! SEC!" rang out through the Louisiana Superdome. The conference had won consecutive national titles for the first time since winning three in a row from 1978 to 1980.

There would be many more to come.

2009 BCS NATIONAL CHAMPIONSHIP GAME: FLORIDA VS. OKLAHOMA

The first-ever meeting between Florida and Oklahoma came on the biggest possible stage. Both of the most recent two Heisman Trophy winners—Florida's Tim Tebow and Oklahoma's Sam Bradford—were expected to carve up the opposing defenses in their battle for the national title.

Urban Meyer's Gators and Bob Stoops's Sooners were scoring a combined 99 points per game. Oklahoma had been particularly nasty, scoring 60-plus points in five consecutive contests entering the prizefight in Miami.

Analysts had seen the SEC dominate two consecutive title games, and they expected more.

In a moment of foreshadowing on the opening drive, Bradford tossed a deep pass down the left sideline. Receiver Manuel Johnson reached for it, but Florida safety Major Wright planted his helmet into Johnson's chin and leveled him with a vicious hit, leaving the Sooner gasping for air on the turf as the Gators bench screamed in delight.

So it went for both offenses in the first half. Florida defensive coordinator Charlie Strong and his Oklahoma counterpart, Brent Venables, were supposed to be helpless. Instead, they decided the game. Tebow threw two interceptions in the first 23 minutes, matching his total from the entire regular season. Bradford tossed a pair as well, his first in more than two months.

With the score tied 7–7 at halftime, Tebow tried to light a fire under his teammates with an impassioned speech.

"He came to us, said he was sorry, and said we were going to come out and run the ball down the field and win this game," wideout David Nelson explained.

Florida leaders Tim Tebow (left) and Urban Meyer (right) hug after winning a second national championship in three seasons. The Gators' impressive 2008 run began with "The Promise," a soul-stirring press conference given by Tebow in September. AP PHOTO/CHRIS O'MEARA

Unable to slice up Oklahoma through the air, Tebow began dragging Florida toward victory with his legs. When he ripped off a 12-yard run through the heart of the defense, he wildly pumped his fist and threw up his hands, imploring the Miami crowd to get back into the game.

The frenzy was like spinach for Popeye. Tebow kept the ball moving with runs of 4, 15, 12, and 6 yards before Percy Harvin punched in the go-ahead score.

Following an Oklahoma touchdown that made it 14–14, Harvin ran circles around the Sooners. He collected 64 combined yards on two runs to open the following drive, putting Florida in position for a go-ahead field goal.

Then—after Florida safety Ahmad Black turned an Oklahoma completion into an interception by stealing the ball away from Juaquin Iglesias—it was Tebow's turn again.

Back in September, Florida's national title hopes were very much in doubt when the Gators fell to unranked Ole Miss in an upset loss that was featured on the cover of *Sports Illustrated*. After the game, a red-eyed Tebow had made what became known as the Promise.

"I promise you one thing," he said at the postgame podium. "A lot of good will come out of this. You will never see any player in the entire country play as hard as I will play the rest of the season. You will never see someone push the rest of the team as hard as I will push somebody the rest of the season. You will never see a team play harder than we will the rest of the season. God bless."

Now he had the football in his hands and a chance to deliver.

On first down from the Florida 24-yard line, he ran the option to his right and then shoveled the ball inside to tight end Aaron Hernandez for 13 yards. On third-and-12 from his own 35, he rolled left and hit wideout Riley Cooper for 17 yards and a crucial first down.

He completed a 29-yarder to David Nelson. A 4-yarder to Harvin. A 9-yarder to Hernandez. By the time it was second-and-goal from the Oklahoma 4-yard line, Tebow and the Gators had run nearly seven minutes off the clock.

His ensuing touchdown pass—a patented "jump" throw—to Nelson gave Florida a 24–14 cushion.

"And Superman strikes again!" said FOX announcer Thom Brennaman.

When Tebow iced the game with a first-down run on the Gators' next possession, he received the first unsportsmanlike penalty of his career. Replays showed he had let his emotions runneth over and directed a few overenthusiastic "Gator Chomps" toward the Sooners.

He had accounted for 340 of Florida's 480 yards and solidified himself as the best player in the country.

"I'm still not sure I can name the nation's best team," wrote Bill Plaschke of the *Los Angeles Times*. "But I'm absolutely positive of its biggest star, that being the Florida Gators quarterback who looks like a

Four Horseman, acts like Seven Blocks of Granite and talks like Knute Rockne."

Tebow's teammates were still thinking about the promise the quarterback had made in September.

"You know, he didn't have to do that," Harvin said. "Nobody ever does that, and it changed everything. From that moment on, we climbed on his back."

2010 BCS NATIONAL CHAMPIONSHIP GAME: ALABAMA VS. TEXAS

Alabama's latest dynasty began in the same building where the first one did. The Crimson Tide was playing in the Rose Bowl nearly a century after the program's watershed win over Washington, and 64 years after its most recent postseason appearance in Pasadena.

Speaking of history, there was a major problem: 'Bama was there to play Texas, a team it had faced eight times but never defeated.

That didn't deter the oddsmakers from making the Tide a 4-point favorite.

Nick Saban's team had not allowed a 100-yard rusher in more than two years, and Mack Brown's squad wasn't going to break that streak. None of the Longhorns backs had come anywhere close to hitting 1,000 on the season, as Brown preferred to just put the football in quarterback Colt McCoy's hands.

McCoy, a senior, had torn up the Big 12 since replacing Vince Young in 2006. Entering the national title game, he and the 'Horns had won 17 consecutive games and 26 of their past 27.

Nick Saban and his "NFL team without a salary cap," as the *Chicago Tribune* called the Crimson Tide, were streaking without any caveats: 'Bama was 13–0 and had just knocked off No. 1 Florida in a convincing SEC title game win.

It was 'Bama that landed a knockout blow in the first quarter.

Fewer than four minutes into the game, McCoy ran an option play to the left. He tucked the ball, cut upfield, and took a full-speed wallop from 280-pound defensive tackle Marcell Dareus. While the hit looked fairly normal, it was the most important play of the game. McCoy's throwing

Alabama defensive lineman Marcell Dareus collects an interception during the 2010 BCS National Championship Game. The Alabama defense knocked Texas star Colt McCoy out of the game and hounded backup Garrett Gilbert.
AP PHOTO/MARK J. TERRILL

arm had suffered severe nerve damage and gone completely numb. He walked to the sideline and took a knee as trainers swarmed him.

In came freshman Garrett Gilbert, a former five-star prospect from Austin who had thrown just 26 career passes.

Texas would have been better off putting in the long-dead corpse of Stephen F. Austin, at least for the first two quarters. Gilbert completed just 1 of his first 10 passes for a grand total of minus-4 yards. His first interception led to a 'Bama field goal, and his second one was taken to the house by Dareus just before halftime.

Alabama, despite an unimpressive offensive effort, had a 24–6 lead and figured to keep Texas off the scoreboard over the final 30 minutes.

But the Crimson Tide O continued to struggle, and Gilbert eventually began moving the ball. He hit Jordan Shipley for a 44-yard touchdown near the end of the third quarter, and then found Shipley again for a 28-yard touchdown with 6:15 remaining in the game. A successful 2-point throw cut the Alabama advantage to 24–21, and the Tide was forced to punt the ball away for the fourth time in five drives.

An ABC graphic illustrated how much Gilbert had improved over the course of the game, and announcers Brent Musburger and Kirk Herbstreit detected a new sense of confidence from the freshman.

"What a change," Herbstreit said.

On first down from his own 12-yard line, Gilbert dropped back and looked to his right. This was unfortunate for him because it meant he couldn't see Alabama defensive end Eryk Anders screaming off the left edge.

Anders torpedoed into Gilbert's back, the ball came loose, and linebacker Courtney Upshaw recovered it. Moments later, 'Bama running back—and Heisman Trophy winner—Mark Ingram bowled into the end zone for a 10-point lead.

Two more Crimson Tide interceptions in the closing moments gave Alabama its first national title in 17 years.

Quarterback Greg McElroy had completed only 6 of 11 passes for 58 yards, but the Tide's top two running backs (Ingram and Trent Richardson, 100-plus yards each) had produced enough offense to avoid wasting an exceptional defensive performance. 'Bama had forced five turnovers and held Texas to 276 total yards on the night.

"Yes, Alabama, this season's version of the Crimson Tide could have been your dad's Crimson Tide, too," read the Associated Press recap. "Or Bear Bryant's."

That last line was a bit of unintentional foreshadowing. The rest of college football knew Alabama was "back," but no one knew the word dynasty would soon be thrown around.

2011 BCS NATIONAL CHAMPIONSHIP GAME: AUBURN VS. OREGON

There were four lead changes, a game-tying 2-point conversion, and an astonishing last-minute play that immediately found its way into BCS lore. But it's fair to say Auburn-Oregon was a disappointment.

"The way it looks now, the BCS championship game will last longer than 'The Godfather Trilogy,'" the *Birmingham News*'s Mark McCarter had written all the way back in late November. "The final score will seem more like an NBA All-Star Game . . . All in all, it could be absolutely entertaining theater."

South Carolina coach Steve Spurrier had predicted a 60–55 Auburn win—a "reasonable projection," noted the *New York Times*—and Las Vegas had set the over-under in the mid-70s.

Fitting, then, that two offenses that were each averaging more than 40 points per game—one with an already-legendary Heisman Trophy winner, one with a quarterback and running back duo that had totaled nearly 60 touchdowns—would fall on their faces immediately after kickoff.

The seemingly unstoppable Ducks went three-and-out to open the game. Ditto for Cam Newton and the Tigers on their first drive. Then, an interception. And another one. And another one.

More than 15 minutes ticked off the clock before Oregon finally took a 3–0 lead.

The breakthrough seemed to ignite Newton, the Tigers quarterback who had won the Heisman Trophy after one of the greatest offensive seasons in SEC history. Nursing an injured back, he went 5-of-5 for 67 yards and a go-ahead touchdown toss to Kodi Burns on the ensuing drive.

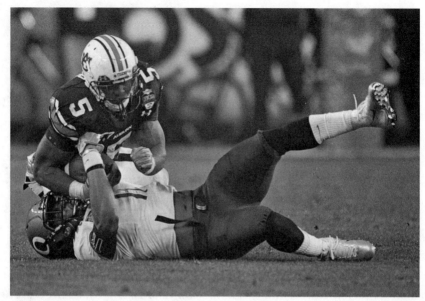

The tackle that wasn't: Auburn running back Michael Dyer's knee does not touch the ground here, so he gets up and scampers for a crucial 37-yard gain. His play put the Tigers in position for their first national title in 53 years.
AP PHOTO/MARK J. TERRILL

Oregon's two-headed monster of quarterback Darron Thomas and running back LaMichael James countered with an 8-yard touchdown connection, and Newton responded with a 30-yard scoring pass to Emory Blake. Finally, the game seemed to be reaching its potential.

And then . . . nothing.

Nearly two full quarters went by without another touchdown as the defenses forced a punt, turnover on downs, or traditional turnover on eight consecutive drives.

Auburn led 19–11 with 4:54 remaining when Oregon linebacker Casey Matthews dove after a scrambling Newton and punched the football out of the quarterback's right hand. Oregon recovered, and eight plays later, Thomas hit James for another short touchdown. The Ducks then converted a 2-point pass from Thomas to Jeff Maehl that tied the game, 19–19.

Overtime appeared likely when Auburn running back Michael Dyer took a first-down carry on the following possession. The true freshman from Little Rock was wrestled to the ground near the Auburn 46-yard line, and many fans turned their attention to the next play.

But Dyer, sensing that his knee had not touched the ground, popped back up. He paused for a moment, then heard his sideline screaming at him.

"I didn't hear a whistle and I was looking at them like, 'What's going on?'" Dyer said. "The team was yelling for me to come on. So, I took off."

In a flash he was down the sideline for a 37-yard gain.

A nation of skeptical viewers shouted for a video review. Surely his knee or elbow had hit the ground at some point?

But the tape was clear: Dyer had rolled over the Oregon defender, keeping everything but his feet and his left hand off the grass. His run was legitimate, and Auburn suddenly had the ball in field goal range with a chance to bleed out the clock.

The Tigers did just that, and junior Wes Bynum drilled an 19-yard kick as time ran out.

Auburn's triumph had not been the classic many expected, but it gave the Tigers their first ring in 53 years and the SEC its fifth consecutive national title. Newton was a national champion in his only season on the Plains.

"I guarantee you five or six months ago that nobody would've bet their last dollar to say that," he said. "We're smiling right now. We got the last laugh."

2012 BCS NATIONAL CHAMPIONSHIP GAME: ALABAMA VS. LSU

In a pleasant plot twist, Bowl Championship Series leadership didn't appear to need a fire extinguisher in November 2011. Louisiana State was a consensus choice at No. 1. Oklahoma State was an excellent option at No. 2, and the undefeated Cowboys were favored to beat Iowa State by four touchdowns in their final contest.

But the morning of the game, OSU got word of a tragedy: two athletics employees had died in a plane crash the night before. Head women's basketball coach Kurt Budke and his assistant coach, Miranda Serna, perished alongside pilot Olin Branstetter and his wife, Paula. The news dominated sports coverage throughout the following day and had a strong effect on the Cowboys locker room in Ames.

"Honestly, the last thing that anybody wants to do, really, is play a game," coach Mike Gundy said.

Oklahoma State fell to Iowa State, 37–31, in double overtime. The loss created an opening for No. 3 Alabama to sneak back into the title picture, and the Crimson Tide eventually nipped the Cowboys for a title shot by 0.0086 points in the final BCS rankings.

So, five years after the Big Ten was denied an Ohio State-Michigan rematch, the SEC—winner of five consecutive national titles—was gifted a second version of Alabama-LSU.

The first tilt had been heavily hyped and unfortunately clunky, a "Game of the Century" that featured zero touchdowns and a seemingly infinite amount of field goal attempts as LSU topped 'Bama, 9-6. Fans outside of the South—heck, most people outside Tuscaloosa—had no interest in seeing the Crimson Tide and Tigers meet again that January.

Regardless of anyone's preference, it was Nick Saban and Les Miles who brought their teams to New Orleans for an all-SEC title game.

Few points were expected, and few points materialized.

A nation's fears were realized as the field goals began to fly. Alabama's Jeremy Shelley hit from 23, 34, and 41—and had a 41-yarder blocked—as the Crimson Tide built a 9–0 halftime lead. Louisiana State scraped together just 33 yards of offense in the process.

The Alabama defense, which featured more than a dozen future NFL draft picks, was treating the Tigers offense like a Pop Warner squad. On one third-quarter play, LSU quarterback Jordan Jefferson was so flustered that he shoveled a forward pass toward a running back who was no longer looking his direction. 'Bama linebacker C. J. Mosley collected the errant attempt and returned it to the LSU 27-yard line.

Shelley missed another kick on the ensuing drive, but he also connected from 35 and 44 to extend the Tide cushion to 15–0 entering the fourth.

By the time 'Bama running back Trent Richardson raced down the left sideline for the game-clinching 34-yard touchdown with 4:36 remaining, LSU had crossed midfield just one time. No one had been expecting much from the Tigers O, but its ineffectiveness was stunning nonetheless.

Saban had his second national title at Alabama and third overall. Unlike the Gatorade bath he received two years prior—when the players accidentally bashed him on the head with the bucket and he responded with the sourest expression in the history of championship celebrations—this one went smoothly.

"The players improved in terms of their ability to deliver," Saban said. "I improved on my ability to accept, and everybody was happy."

2013 BCS NATIONAL CHAMPIONSHIP GAME: ALABAMA VS. NOTRE DAME

It's tough to nail down when, exactly, Nick Saban's powers reached their peak, but January 2013 is a great guess. Saban's Crimson Tide had won two of the past three national titles and was in position to win another. Alabama was so good that—despite having lost a game to Johnny Manziel and Texas A&M in November—it was considered by many sportsbooks to be a 10-point favorite over undefeated and No. 1-ranked Notre Dame.

It didn't much matter that the Fighting Irish had shut down four ranked teams and slapped around rival USC at the Coliseum to close their regular season, or that they had the best defensive player in the country, or that their fans would outnumber the Tide's in Miami; they were sacrificial lambs.

When ABC's Brent Musburger unleashed his trademark "You are looking live at . . ." line to open the broadcast, he might as well have finished it with "the calm before the bloodbath."

Alabama drove 82 yards for a game-opening touchdown run by Eddie Lacy. It forced a punt, then drove 51 yards for another score, capped by a short pass from AJ McCarron to tight end Michael Williams. Another Notre Dame punt, another Alabama touchdown drive, this one 80 yards long and punctuated by a 1-yard T. J. Yeldon plunge.

Alabama quarterback AJ McCarron throws during a blowout win over Notre Dame in the 2013 BCS National Championship Game. McCarron finished with 4 touchdown passes in the rout. CAL SPORT MEDIA VIA AP IMAGES

Just before halftime, 'Bama completed a 71-yard drive with a touchdown pass from McCarron to Lacy.

Saban's team had a 28–0 lead, and America began looking for other things to watch. Those who tuned out knew what they were missing: the ho-hum conclusion of yet another predictable Alabama episode.

'Bama pushed its lead to 35 points with a comically breezy 97-yard drive. Notre Dame's first points came more than 40 minutes into the game, and the Irish's slim hopes were immediately rebuffed by a second consecutive touchdown pass from McCarron to freshman wideout Amari Cooper.

The Tide cruised to a 42–14 final advantage, with McCarron (four passing touchdowns) and Lacy (146 rushing yards) providing the headlines against All-America linebacker Manti Te'o and one of the country's highest-rated defenses.

Meanwhile, the Tide front had allowed just 32 rushing yards in the demolition. Saban's defense had exorcised some demons in Alabama's second-ever win over Notre Dame, earning long-awaited bragging rights for the Tide fans who had suffered through several painful losses to the team from South Bend (Bear Bryant was 0–4 vs. the Irish).

"On a flawless South Florida night, Notre Dame players saw a legend emerge in present time," wrote Brian Hamilton of the *Chicago Tribune*. "To their bone-deep disbelief, it was not them."

2016 NATIONAL TITLE GAME: ALABAMA VS. CLEMSON
On September 19, 2015, Alabama's dynasty ended. Several prominent media pundits sent off Nick Saban's glory years with long-winded explanations and predictions of future turmoil. Here is an incomplete collection:

"There's no greater indicator of a lost dynasty, no more prominent red flag, than ignoring the obvious: this is not the same Alabama program of years gone by."—Matt Hayes, *Sporting News*

"The dynasty argument is about a state of mind, a state of being. That's gone. That no longer exists at Alabama. They have no right to it anymore."—Dan Wolken, *USA Today*

"No one fears Alabama anymore."—Jon Solomon, CBS Sports

"They have a Nick Saban problem at Alabama."—Joel Klatt, FOX Sports

Alabama's 43–37 loss to Ole Miss had supposedly reset the SEC's power structure, and 'Bama was left for dead in the national title race.

That slowly changed (and the apologies came trickling in) as the Crimson Tide destroyed No. 8 Georgia, No. 9 Texas A&M, and No. 2 LSU en route to a College Football Playoff berth and a 38–0 massacre of Big Ten champion Michigan State in the semifinal.

The Alabama dynasty was as alive as ever when it arrived in Glendale, Arizona, for a shot at its fourth national title in the past seven seasons. Its roadblock: the No. 1 Clemson Tigers, coached by former 'Bama wide receiver—and 1992 champion—Dabo Swinney.

Clemson had run the table and dealt a 'Bama-esque knockout blow to Oklahoma in the opposite semifinal. Junior quarterback Deshaun Watson was a dual-threat nightmare who was on his way to a historic final tally of 4,000-plus passing yards and 1,000-plus rushing yards. He had fallen short in the Heisman Trophy race, however.

Alabama tight end O. J. Howard soars toward one of his 2 touchdowns in a thrilling 2016 national title game vs. Clemson. Rarely used in the passing game, Howard shocked the Tigers with 208 receiving yards. AP PHOTO/DAVID J. PHILLIP

The winner: Alabama running back Derrick Henry, an inordinately tall runner from tiny Yulee, Florida, who was built like a linebacker (a big linebacker). Henry had already set the SEC single-season rushing record, passing Herschel Walker's 34-year-old mark in a conference title game win over Florida. He entered the national championship matchup with more than 2,000 yards to his name, and quickly added to his total.

Facing third-and-1 from midfield midway through the first quarter, Henry took an inside handoff from quarterback Jake Coker, bounced to the right, and raced through the arms of a Clemson defensive back. He was off, and so was the heavyweight matchup.

The Tigers provided a quick response, racing down the field to set up a 31-yard passing touchdown from Watson to Hunter Renfrow. Following a missed 'Bama field goal, Clemson's quarterback began digging up those old "dead dynasty" fears that Crimson Tide fans had shelved for four months.

Watson scrambled for 11 yards. He threw for 24. He threw for 20. Then, as the first quarter ran out, he threw another touchdown strike to Renfrow. Leading 14–7, Clemson had already put up a bigger fight than any of Alabama's previous three national title opponents.

"We stand toe-to-toe with everybody in the country," Swinney said afterward. "This program doesn't take a backseat to anybody."

'Bama offensive coordinator Lane Kiffin had a surprise in store for the upstart Tigers.

Tight end O. J. Howard typically served as a run-blocker and decoy. And that's apparently all Clemson expected from him, because Howard found himself running wide open with a 53-yard touchdown catch that made it 21–14 Alabama in the third quarter.

It was Howard's first score in more than two years.

Alabama linebacker Rashaan Evans sacks Clemson quarterback Deshaun Watson. The Tigers quarterback put on a scintillating performance in the loss, totaling 478 yards and 4 touchdowns. AP PHOTO/CHRIS CARLSON

"I've got to wait and be patient," he had told the ESPN crew days before the game. "But when I get a chance, I've gotta be sure I take it."

Clemson had no time for feel-good moments. Watson and the Tigers quickly took back the lead with a field goal and a 1-yard touchdown run by Wayne Gallman.

The teams traded four punts, then Coker found ArDarius Stewart for a 38-yard pickup on third-and-11 that led to a short Adam Griffith field goal.

Viewers might have remembered Griffith as the unfortunate soul on the wrong end of Auburn's "Kick Six" in the 2013 Iron Bowl. He was Polish immigrant, the son of adoptive American parents who tried kicking footballs on a lark and was—after one 57-yard field goal attempt that fell short on that crazy November night—labeled a failure.

He had become permanently attached to one of the greatest moments in college football history, and it wasn't a good thing.

At the team hotel before the Clemson game, Saban had told Griffith the Crimson Tide would likely attempt an onside kick that night. When, in the first half, coaches noticed Clemson lining up in the same formation they'd seen on film, it was decided: Alabama would use the onside at some point.

A 24–24 game with 10:34 remaining was apparently the perfect time.

It was up to Griffith to approach the football as if he were going to kick it deep, then break off his pattern at the last moment and loft the ball toward the right sideline, where cornerback Marlon Humphrey was supposed to snag it. In practice, the move was less than foolproof; teammates later claimed Humphrey "always drops it," and that the redshirt freshman had failed to corral the ball during the team's final practice before the title game.

With a potential national championship less than a quarter away, Saban's plan worked to perfection. Griffith hit the kick beautifully, and Humphrey sprinted underneath it to give back possession to the Crimson Tide.

It was the call of the season, and 'Bama quickly capitalized.

On second-and-11 from the Alabama 49-yard line, Coker dropped back to pass and saw Howard running wide open again. He lofted a touch pass to the tight end, who sped into the end zone for his second touch-down of the game.

Clemson responded with a field goal, but Alabama's special teams struck again. Kick returner Kenyan Drake sprinted around the Tigers' coverage unit and sped down the left sideline, diving past one final tackler and crashing into the pylon for a 95-yard score. 'Bama had a 38–27 lead with seven and a half minutes remaining.

Watson was not done, though. He completed passes of 14 and 39 yards and then found Artavis Scott for a 15-yard score with 4:40 left.

With the Alabama defense operating more like a turnstile, its offense was forced to preserve a 38–33 lead. And it did so with another long con-nection between Coker and Howard, this one for 63 yards to the Clem-son 14-yard line. The unheralded tight end now had five receptions for 208 yards, and the dejected Tigers defense allowed Henry to impart the kill shot with a 1-yard touchdown run.

Watson managed one final touchdown drive, but Clemson failed to convert the ensuing onside kick, and Coker kneeled down to end the game.

Alabama's 45–40 win produced a rare celebratory dance—including an even rarer collection of schoolboy grins—by Saban. Some wondered if the 64-year-old might be ready to announce his retirement. Resurrecting dynasties is exhausting work, after all, and Alabama's fourth title in seven seasons was already unprecedented in the post-1936 poll era.

But those ready to wrap up the accomplishment with a bow were missing the point; for Saban, it would soon be about No. 5 (or No. 6 . . . or No. 7).

"I think as long as he's in Alabama," Coker said," Alabama is going to be up at the top."

2017 NATIONAL TITLE GAME: ALABAMA VS. GEORGIA

"Tua Time" was never supposed to arrive. Nick Saban did everything in his power to keep it from happening. And yet, with 30 minutes remaining in the national championship game, the legendary coach buckled.

Saban's longtime starter, Jalen Hurts, had failed to develop as a passer. The Crimson Tide's aerial offense had been the team's Achilles' heel for

Alabama coach Nick Saban soaks in his sixth national championship. The Crimson Tide's overtime win against Georgia will be remembered for Saban's decision to bench starting quarterback Jalen Hurts in favor of true freshman Tua Tagovailoa. AP PHOTO/DAVID J. PHILLIP

the better part of two seasons, especially in a close loss to Clemson in the national title game the previous January.

The basic scouting report: Hurts was an outstanding runner, but struggled to make plays with his arm on third-and-10.

So, in the most important game of the season, against former 'Bama defensive coordinator Kirby Smart and an elite Georgia team, with another national title on the line and a 13–0 deficit on the Mercedes Benz Stadium scoreboard . . . it was time for a change.

Alabama being Alabama, there was a five-star recruit biding his time on the bench: Tua Tagovailoa, a Hawaiian wunderkind from the same high school as former Oregon star and Heisman Trophy winner Marcus

Mariota. The southpaw was considered one of America's best-throwing prospects in the class of 2017, if not the best. And when he saw bits and pieces of playing time in his first season, he dazzled.

There had been rumblings that Tagovailoa felt he had outplayed Hurts in practice for much of the season. Former Alabama offensive coordinator—and current Florida Atlantic coach—Lane Kiffin claimed as much in the days following Tagovailoa's coming-out party.

And what a party it was.

With 'Bama trailing 13–0 on his second drive, Tagovailoa completed four consecutive passes—including three straight to Henry Ruggs III—to get the Crimson Tide onto the scoreboard.

Trailing 20–13 with a little less than seven minutes remaining in the game, he led an eight-play, 66-yard drive that featured completions of 17 and 20 yards before his best play of regulation. Facing fourth-and-4 from the Georgia 7-yard line, Tagovailoa took a shotgun snap. He looked to his right, then, moving to his left, bailed backwards out of the pocket. In a flash he fired a pass toward well-covered running back Najee Harris in the end zone. But star wide receiver Calvin Ridley stepped in front of the mess and snatched the ball for the tying touchdown.

Walk-on Tide kicker Andy Pappanastos missed the potential game-winning 36-yard field goal, so Tagovailoa was once again called upon in overtime.

It was in that extra period when he succumbed to a major freshman mistake: he took an ugly sack that pushed 'Bama back to the Georgia 41-yard line.

"A disastrous first-down play!" shouted ESPN's Chris Fowler.

Down 23–20, there was no need to play it safe; Pappanastos couldn't be counted on to tie the game from deep. A touchdown would win it. So offensive coordinator Brian Daboll called one of the simplest plays he had: "Seattle."

Translation: everybody go deep. If Georgia "rolled" its safeties toward the right sideline, it was Tagovailoa's job to look off the "centerfielder" to one side of the field and throw it to the other.

The teams lined up. Indeed, the 'Dawgs safeties were cheating. All-SEC senior Dominick Sanders—who had recently matched the school's career record for interceptions—was inching toward the middle of the formation. The freshman quarterback would need to keep him there.

Tagovailoa took the snap as his receivers shot toward the end zone. He kept his eyes glued on the slot receiver running a deep post, freezing Sanders in the middle of the field. At the end of his drop, Tagovailoa snapped his head around and fired a dart to the left side of the end zone. He hadn't even looked at the coverage; he knew fellow freshman receiver Devonta Smith would be open.

With no safety over the top, Smith had no one between him and the football. Suddenly, improbably, the game was over, and Alabama was the national champion for the 17th time. This was the latest title notch on Saban's belt, extending what Associated Press reporter Ralph D. Russo called "the greatest dynasty that college football has ever seen."

Hurts, the benched quarterback, celebrated with the kid that replaced him and kept his composure during a headline-garnering postgame TV interview on ESPN.

In the locker room, he had nothing but respect for Saban's decision to unleash Tua Time.

"It was an executive decision," Hurts said, "and it was a good one."

Tagovailoa, who finished with 166 yards and three touchdown passes, agreed.

"I don't know how Coach Saban found me all the way in Hawaii from Alabama," he said. "Thank God he found me and we're here right now."

FULL LIST OF CLAIMED NATIONAL TITLES BY SEC SCHOOLS

Year	School	Record	Coach
1917	Georgia Tech*	9–0	John Heisman
1925	Alabama*	10–0	Wallace Wade
1926	Alabama*	9–0–1	Wallace Wade
1928	Georgia Tech*	10–0	William Alexander
1930	Alabama*	10–0	Wallace Wade
1934	Alabama	10–0	Frank Thomas
1938	Tennessee	11–0	Robert Neyland
1940	Tennessee	10–1	Robert Neyland
1941	Alabama**	9–2	Frank Thomas
1942	Georgia	11–1	Wally Butts
1950	Tennessee	11–1	Robert Neyland
1950	Kentucky**	11–1	Paul "Bear" Bryant
1951	Tennessee	11–1	Robert Neyland
1952	Georgia Tech	12–0	Bobby Dodd
1957	Auburn	10–0	Ralph "Shug" Jordan
1958	LSU	11–0	Paul Dietzel
1959	Ole Miss	10–1	Johnny Vaught
1960	Ole Miss	10–0–1	Johnny Vaught
1961	Alabama	11–0	Paul "Bear" Bryant
1962	Ole Miss	10–0	Johnny Vaught
1964	Alabama	10–1	Paul "Bear" Bryant
1965	Alabama	9–1–1	Paul "Bear" Bryant
1967	Tennessee**	9–2	Doug Dickey

1973	Alabama	11–1	Paul "Bear" Bryant
1978	Alabama	11–1	Paul "Bear" Bryant
1979	Alabama	12–0	Paul "Bear" Bryant
1980	Georgia	12–0	Vince Dooley
1992	Alabama	13–0	Gene Stallings
1996	Florida	12–1	Steve Spurrier
1998	Tennessee	13–0	Phillip Fulmer
2003	LSU	13–1	Nick Saban
2006	Florida	13–1	Urban Meyer
2007	LSU	13–1	Les Miles
2008	Florida	13–1	Urban Meyer
2009	Alabama	14–0	Nick Saban
2010	Auburn	14–0	Gene Chizik
2011	Alabama	12–1	Nick Saban
2012	Alabama	13–1	Nick Saban
2015	Alabama	14–1	Nick Saban
2017	Alabama	13–1	Nick Saban

*Title earned before formation of SEC in 1933
**Particularly dubious claim

INDEX

INDEX

African-American players, 13
vs. Alabama, 25–50
coaches, 33
vs. Florida, 88–89
vs. Georgia, 52, 63, 68–70,
 101–2
vs. LSU, 64–66, 98–100,
 100–101
vs. Oregon, 219–21
vs. Tennessee, 147–49
winning streak, 108

Baker, Robert, 101
Barfield, Wayne, 89
Barker, Jay, 19, 143, 147
Barron, Mark, 128–29
Bates, Bill, 16, 110, 200
BCS National Championship
 Game, 105, 167
 1999, 152
 2007, 20–23
 2008, 210–13
 2009, 213–16
 2010, 216–19
 2011, 219–21
 2012, 165, 221–23
 2013, 223–25
Beasley, Fred, 102, 149
Beckwith, Darry, 126
Belichick, Bill, 124, 125
Bell, Albert, 37
Bell, Kenny, 134
Bell, Robert, 15
Bell, T'Sharvan, 43
Bellamy, Davin, 139

Bellard, Emory, 58
Belue, Buck, 56, 57, 198,
 199, 202
Belue, Deion, 133
Bendross, Jesse, 30
Bielema, Bret, 71
Birmingham, DeCori, 64,
 112, 116
Bisceglia, Steve, 29
Black, Ahmad, 215
Blackledge, Todd, 155
Blake, Emory, 220
Blakeney, Larry, 88
Blankenship, Rodrigo, 138
"Bluegrass Miracle," 60–62
"Bo Over the Top," 30, 36, 38–39
Bobo, Mike, 101–2, 165
Boeckman, Todd, 212
Booth, Albie "Little Boy Blue," 77
Bowden, Bobby, 32, 103, 202,
 203–4, 205, 207
Bowden, Terry, 100, 102, 148, 149
Boyd, Willard "Red," 180
Bradford, Sam, 160, 213
Bray, Jayson, 101, 149
Brindise, Noah, 103, 104
Britt, Charlie, 52
Brooks, Rich, 116
Brown, Curtis, 143
Brown, Fred, 52
Brown, Johnny Mack, 7
Brown, Mack, 216
Browndyke, David, 99
Broyles, Frank, 9, 191
Bruce Bolton, 196

INDEX

INDEX

ABOUT THE AUTHOR

Alex Martin Smith is a journalist living in Nashville. He has primarily reported for the *Atlanta Journal-Constitution* and its college football vertical SEC Country since moving to Music City in 2014. Smith previously served on staff at MLB.com and the *St. Paul Pioneer Press*. A native of the Minneapolis area, he studied journalism at the University of Missouri–Columbia. He lives with his wife, Bridget, near Vanderbilt University.

Which games and legends did we miss? There were some close calls. Read more—and access the full *SEC Football's Greatest Games* bibliography—online at SECFootballBook.com.